The Tragedy of William Jennings Bryan

The Tragedy of William Jennings Bryan

Constitutional Law and the Politics of Backlash

Gerard N. Magliocca

Yale UNIVERSITY PRESS NEW HAVEN & LONDON

Yale University Press books may be purchased in quantity for educational, business,
or promotional use. For information, please e-mail sales.press@yale.edu (U.S. office)
or sales@yaleup.co.uk (U.K. office).

Set in Janson type by Newgen North America.
Printed in the United States of America.

Library of Congress Cataloging-in-Publication Data

Magliocca, Gerard N.
The tragedy of William Jennings Bryan : constitutional law and the politics of
backlash / Gerard N. Magliocca.
p. cm.
Includes bibliographical references and index.
ISBN 978-0-300-15314-9 (alk. paper)
1. Constitutional history—United States. 2. United States—Politics and
government—1865–1933. 3. Bryan, William Jennings, 1860–1925. I. Title.
KF4541.M273 2011
342.7302′9—dc22
2010039781

A catalogue record for this book is available from the British Library.

♾ This paper meets the requirements of ANSI/NISO Z39.48-1992.

10 9 8 7 6 5 4 3 2 1

For Guido Calabresi, who made all of this possible

The humblest citizen in all the land, when clad in the armor of a righteous cause, is stronger than all the hosts of error.

—William Jennings Bryan

Contents

Acknowledgments   ix

Introduction: On Constitutional Failure   1

ONE

Constructing Reconstruction   8

TWO

The Rise of Populism   28

THREE

Resistance North and South   48

FOUR

The Supreme Court Intervenes   69

FIVE

The Election of 1896   98

Contents

SIX

A New Constitutional Regime 116

SEVEN

The Progressive Correction 133

Conclusion: What Is Constitutional Failure? 149

Notes 155
Bibliography 213
Index 229

Acknowledgments

Writing one book was so much fun that I decided to write another. I am reluctant to call this one a sequel, as everyone knows that a sequel rarely tops the original. A better description is Norma Desmond's line in *Sunset Boulevard:* she was not making a comeback; it was a return.

Let me start by thanking Michael O'Malley, Mary Pasti, Niahm Cunningham, and Yale University Press for their support and confidence. I owe a special debt to Bruce Ackerman, Barry Friedman, John Hill, Rick Pildes, Mike Pitts, Tom Shakow, and Amanda Tyler for reading the draft manuscript and offering their thoughtful comments. Debra Denslaw and Kiyoshi Otsu provided vital assistance in gathering the photographs that help make the book come alive. The law journals that allowed me to reprint parts of my previously published work here, and whose officers edited those papers, also deserve my gratitude. The articles are "Why Did the Incorporation of the Bill of Rights Fail in the Late Nineteenth Century?" *Minnesota Law Review* 94 (2009): 102–139, and "Constitutional False Positives and the Populist Moment," *Notre Dame Law Review* 81 (2006): 821–888.

Finally, I want to salute my colleagues at Indiana University School of Law–Indianapolis, whose friendship and encouragement is invaluable, and the scholars at the Roosevelt Study Center in Middelburg, The Netherlands, who hosted me during a delightful sabbatical when I ended up thinking a lot about this book, helped along by lots of herring.

On Constitutional Failure

When you strike at a king, you must *kill* him.
—RALPH WALDO EMERSON

We learn more from failure than from success. Although this lesson is often a bitter one, everyone eventually learns its truth—everyone, it seems, except constitutional lawyers. Their story of how "We the People" created, amended, and then interpreted the Constitution is an uplifting drama. The Founding Fathers and the miracle that was the Constitutional Convention, the abolition of slavery and Abraham Lincoln's reconstruction of our ideals in the Gettysburg Address, Franklin D. Roosevelt's development of the welfare state to overcome the Great Depression, and the Supreme Court's decisions striking down racial segregation are the pillars of modern legal analysis. Those achievements are clearly worth studying, but what about the close calls that ended in frustration? Their omission from the standard

William Jennings Bryan,
"The Boy Orator of the Platte."
Library of Congress.

narrative creates a distortion in constitutional law no different from what scientists face when their laboratory experiments are incomplete.[1]

The most important constitutional failure that is missing from the professional conversation is the defeat of the Populist Party and its presidential candidate, William Jennings Bryan, in 1896. Today Bryan is remembered mainly for his role in challenging the teaching of evolution in public schools during the infamous Scopes Trial. But in his heyday he was widely acclaimed as the nation's greatest orator, and he carried the banner for liberalism in three presidential campaigns. Because he lost all three of those races (in 1896, 1900, and 1908) and was overshadowed by an even larger personality, we now associate progressive reform and, indeed, the entire political era with Theodore Roosevelt. Nevertheless, a central theme of this book is that Bryan, not the

Rough Rider, was the greatest constitutional figure at the turn of the twentieth century.

The 1890s present a fascinating puzzle for political scientists. Bryan's defeat in 1896 at the hands of William McKinley is commonly described as a "realigning" election that marked a major and long-lasting shift in public policy. Yet David Mayhew, a scholar at Yale, recently challenged this consensus by arguing that the 1896 result was not significant, in part because no dramatic legislative changes occurred after McKinley's victory.[2] Mayhew calls this inaction the "third rail of the realignments genre" and concludes that "the 1890s pose a basic interpretive difficulty" for the whole idea that there are political realignments.[3] Uncertainty about the meaning of the 1890s also appears in the work of Stephen Skowronek, the author of an influential theory on the presidency. Though his analysis succeeds in categorizing the presidents and reveals a pattern to their behavior across different time periods, the man in the White House during the 1896 campaign—Grover Cleveland—is an enigma. Skowronek observes that President Cleveland, who openly opposed Bryan's election even though he was a fellow Democrat, "found himself strangely at odds with the burgeoning new opposition movement, and the upshot was the most perplexing leadership performance in American history."[4]

A similar mystery surrounds constitutional law during the 1890s. Prior to that decade, the Supreme Court refused to hold that the Fourteenth Amendment—which guarantees the privileges or immunities of citizens, due process of law, and the equal protection of the laws—imposed limits on state regulation of property and contract rights. In 1897 the Justices changed course and held that the Due Process Clause of the amendment secured a "liberty of contract," which launched an era of heightened judicial scrutiny of economic legislation that continued until the 1930s.[5] Well into the 1890s, the Justices expressed support for extending the substantive parts of the Bill of Rights (such as protection from cruel and unusual punishment) to the states.[6] But in 1900 the Court held that no part of the Bill of Rights other than the Takings Clause was "incorporated" against the states, a position that remained influential for decades.[7] Throughout the first century of the republic, cases on congressional power did not rely on the Commerce Clause.[8] During the 1890s, though, the Commerce Clause became the focal point for judicial inquiries into whether Congress could regulate private conduct.[9] Similarly, the Justices never struck down a federal tax as unconstitutional before 1895, but in that year they suddenly concluded that the Constitution imposed a substantial barrier to a federal income tax.[10] Before 1895, Chief Justice John Marshall's opinion in *Marbury v. Madison* was not considered especially significant and was never cited by the Court to invalidate a federal statute. In the 1896 presidential campaign, however, *Marbury* was celebrated, and it assumed its modern form as a great case.[11] Most important of all, before the 1890s African Americans voted in large numbers across the South, and the comprehensive system of legal segregation that we call Jim Crow did not exist.[12] Just ten years later, compulsory segregation was the law, and African Americans in the old Confederacy were disenfranchised. On all of these questions, lawyers confront the equivalent of Planet X—a hidden force that exerts an observable pull. Since no constitutional amendments were ratified during the 1890s, what explains all of these dramatic changes?

The answer is that there was a powerful backlash against the protest movements associated with the Populists and their goals of wealth redistribution, nationalization of industry, and racial cooperation in the South.[13] William Jennings Bryan's unique constitutional contribution was not in what he did; it was what the fear of him and his followers caused others to do. As *The Nation* said after the 1896 election, "Probably no man in civil life has succeeded in inspiring so much terror, without taking life, as Bryan."[14] This fear spurred the political and legal establishment to fight back by increasing federal constitutional protection for property and contract rights, establishing Jim Crow to prevent an alliance between poor whites and African Americans in the South, and curbing civil liberties to ensure that Populist and labor activists could not rally support. There are many fine studies on the backlash phenomenon, but nobody has done an analysis of what may be the most significant constitutional backlash of all. This book takes up that challenge.

The idea that resistance is a powerful force that shapes the law was an important part of my first book.[15] In discussing the "constitutional generation" led by Andrew Jackson, I argued that there is a cycle in our politics defined by broad popular movements that emerge on a regular basis to challenge constitutional orthodoxy. This call to arms, which occurs about once every thirty years, must overcome fierce opposition from a prior generation of leaders who believe in different ideals and cling to power until they are pushed aside. The pattern of reform, ossification, and rebirth started with the Founders' struggle against the British Empire in the 1770s and continued with Jefferson's "Revolution of 1800," Jacksonian Democracy in the 1830s, Lincoln Republicans in the 1860s, the New Deal in the 1930s, the Civil Rights Movement of the 1960s, the Reagan Revolution in the 1980s, and Barack Obama's victory in 2008.[16] Each of these crusades faced (or, in President Obama's case, is now facing) the kind of intense resistance that met Bryan's forces, but the conservative opposition was always defeated. What makes the 1890s unique is that Bryan lost, and the measures taken against him stayed in place to form a new set of first principles. This constitutional settlement was extraordinarily durable, setting the terms of debate in many areas until the 1960s. Bryan's failure, therefore, led to a legal transformation as profound as the successes that people spend so much time studying.[17]

By closely examining the backlash against Bryanism, I hope to dispel five misconceptions about the late nineteenth century. First, something important did occur as a result of the 1896 race, so the traditional view that that Bryan-McKinley campaign led to a realignment of the electorate is right. Second, the legal doctrines that emerged during this time were not related to the original understanding of the Fourteenth Amendment and did not reflect a logical trend within the cases decided after Reconstruction.[18] Third, the same developments were also not the result of errors (negligent or deliberate) by the Supreme Court. Fourth, the Populist Party was not just the pitchfork-carrying mob depicted by some historians; Populists were in fact legal innovators who made significant contributions to constitutional thought.[19] Finally, the contraction of liberty that crippled so many of our citizens in this period was not inevitable. Millions marched and voted on behalf of a different vision during the 1890s, and their tale should be told.

In sum, this book is about the consequences of failure. A clear implication of Emerson's admonition "When you strike at a king, you must *kill* him" is that the king's vengeance will be fierce if he escapes, and the same point can be made about those who beat back a popular mobilization for constitutional change. The hosts of error, as Bryan called them, are not generous in victory.

ONE

Constructing Reconstruction

> Under the pressure of all the excited feeling growing out of
> the war, our statesmen have still believed that the existence
> of the State with powers for domestic and local government,
> including the regulation of civil rights—the rights of person
> and property—was essential to the perfect working of our
> complex form of government, though they have thought
> proper to impose additional limitations on the States, and
> to confer additional power on that of the Nation.
> —*The Slaughter-House Cases*

Every solution creates another problem. The bloodshed of the
Civil War paved the way for a set of constitutional amendments
that settled forever the issue of whether Americans could hold
slaves or whether those former slaves were citizens of the United
States. At the same time, the amendments raised a new set of
questions about the allocation of authority between the federal government and the states. To see how William Jennings
Bryan's defeat transformed the law during the 1890s, we need
to examine the doctrinal debate that followed Reconstruction.
Accordingly, I focus here on three issues related to the meaning
of the Fourteenth Amendment: (1) whether the states faced additional limits on their authority to regulate property and contract
rights; (2) whether the Bill of Rights now applied to the states;

and (3) to what extent the states were barred from making distinctions based on race. Until the backlash against the Populist coalition, there was no consensus on these three topics. After that backlash, the ambiguities in the Fourteenth Amendment were resolved in line with the views of Bryan's foes.

Slaughter-House and the Interpretive Debate

A natural starting point for any discussion of the Fourteenth Amendment is the *Slaughter-House Cases*, which marked the Supreme Court's first interpretation of the new constitutional language.[1] Some white butchers in New Orleans argued that a state statute granting a butchering monopoly to a corporation that excluded them violated the Privileges or Immunities Clause, the Due Process Clause, and the Equal Protection Clause.[2] The Justices, by a five-to-four vote, rejected that claim in an opinion that touched on most of the basic issues that preoccupied lawyers for the next three decades.

Slaughter-House held that the freedom to work in a trade was not a constitutional right, because the Fourteenth Amendment left the regulation of common-law contract and property rights to the states. The Court reasoned that there was a distinction between national and state citizenship in the Constitution and that only national citizenship rights were protected from state action.[3] Not only did nothing of national importance inhere in the right to work as a butcher, but, as the Court concluded from some cases predating the Fourteenth Amendment, state citizenship "embraces nearly every civil right for the establishment and protection of which organized government is established."[4] To hold otherwise and declare that the common law was absorbed into the Constitution "would constitute this court a perpetual censor upon all legislation of the States" and radically change "the whole theory of the relations of the State and Federal governments to each other and of both governments to the people."[5]

There were three dissenting opinions in *Slaughter-House*, but the most powerful one was by Justice Stephen J. Field, who said that the case presented "nothing less than the question whether the recent amendments to the Federal Constitution protect the citizens of the United States against the deprivation of their common rights by State legislatures."[6] Field observed that the Civil Rights Act of 1866, the antecedent of the Fourteenth Amendment, secured the right "to make and enforce contracts" and the right "to inherit, purchase, lease, sell, hold, or convey real and personal property."[7] He contended that in securing those rights, the act undermined the Court's view that they were not of national significance and supported his position that common-law privileges, including the "right to pursue a lawful employment," did "belong to the citizens of all free governments."[8] If the Fourteenth Amendment did not protect these rights, then "our government will be a republic only in name."[9]

Justice Stephen Field, the lead dissenter in the *Slaughter-House Cases.* Library of Congress.

Slaughter-House did "venture to suggest some" of the rights that were protected by the Fourteenth Amendment "lest it should be said that no such privileges and immunities are to be found if those we have been considering are excluded."[10] In defining the liberties that "owe their existence to the Federal government, its National character, its Constitution, or its laws," the Court wrote that each citizen had the right:

> to come to the seat of government to assert any claim he may have upon that government, to transact any business he may have with it, to seek its protection, to share its offices, to engage in administering its functions. He has the right of free access to its seaports . . . to the subtreasuries, land offices, and courts of justice in the several States.

A citizen also possessed the right:

> to demand the care and protection of the Federal government
> over his life, liberty, and property when on the high seas or
> within the jurisdiction of a foreign government . . . The right
> to peaceably assemble and petition for redress of grievances,
> the privilege of the writ of *habeas corpus* . . . The right to use
> the navigable waters of the United States, however they may
> penetrate the territory of the several States, all rights secured
> to our citizens by treaties with foreign nations . . . One of
> these privileges is conferred by the very article under consid-
> eration. It is that a citizen of the United States can, of his own
> volition, become a citizen of any State of the Union by a *bonâ
> fide* residence therein, with the same rights as other citizens
> of that State. To these may be added the rights secured by the
> thirteenth and fifteen articles of amendment.[11]

This list of federal privileges or immunities is the only guidance
in the opinion about whether the Fourteenth Amendment incorporated (in other words, extended) the Bill of Rights to the states,
which was an important question because the Court held in the
1830s that the Bill applied only to the federal government.[12]

The incorporation issue was not raised by the butchers' claim
about a right to work, but most scholars believe that the analysis in *Slaughter-House* foreclosed the argument that the states
were bound by the first eight amendments.[13] After all, the Court
omitted those fundamental liberties, with the exception of the

Petition Clause, from its discussion of federal privileges or immunities. The omission seems critical because the Justices did see fit to include such trivial items as seaport access and the right to travel. Moreover, Justice Joseph P. Bradley's dissent did mention parts of the Bill of Rights in his definition of national privileges or immunities, which could be construed as implying that the Court's exclusion of them was telling.[14] As a result, one view of *Slaughter-House* is that either the Fourteenth Amendment was declaratory of rights that already existed or it guaranteed nontextual rights inherent in the federal structure.[15]

The other interpretation of the opinion is that its litany of national rights was illustrative rather than exhaustive, and thus the Court did not reject incorporation. The Court's statement that it was suggesting "some" of the privileges or immunities encompassed by the Fourteenth Amendment supports this reading.[16] In fact, some commentators go further and say that the inclusion of the Petition Clause in the key passage should be taken as evidence that the Bill of Rights was incorporated.[17] This conclusion builds on the observation that *Slaughter-House* counted rights specified in the Thirteenth and Fifteenth Amendments (banning slavery and providing for African American suffrage) as national rights, which indicates that privileges in the text—not just structural rights or ones that existed before the ratification of the Fourteenth Amendment—were included.[18]

Nineteenth-century courts did not address these competing interpretations of *Slaughter-House*.[19] Indeed, in no federal case prior to 1900 was the opinion cited as either supporting or rejecting the extension of the Bill of Rights.[20] *Slaughter-House* was cited for the point that state and national citizenship rights were distinct in cases holding that a given part of the Bill of Rights did not apply to the states, but that was not the same as saying that *Slaughter-House* spoke directly to the issue.[21] Given the lack of authority for the proposition that the Court rejected incorporation in 1873, why are so many modern lawyers convinced that this repudiation happened then?

The answer is that nearly thirty years after *Slaughter-House* the Justices declared that the opinion was hostile to incorporation. In *Maxwell v. Dow,* a 1900 case that rejected a claim that the Fourteenth Amendment applied the Sixth Amendment jury trial right to the states,[22] the defendant argued that "all of the provisions in the first ten amendments, so far as they secure and recognize the fundamental rights of the individual as against the exercise of Federal power, are . . . to be regarded as privileges or immunities of a citizen of the United States."[23] In response, the Court quoted *Slaughter-House* at length and concluded that in the section of that opinion on national privileges or immunities, "a right, such as is claimed here, was not mentioned, and we suppose it was regarded as pertaining to the state, and not covered by the amendment."[24] With that statement, *Maxwell* explicitly endorsed the "exhaustive" reading of *Slaughter-House* on incorporation. The critical point is that this endorsement happened after Bryan's 1896 defeat. As we see in chapter 6, that political earthquake turned the meaning of *Slaughter-House* upside down.

Finally, *Slaughter-House* addressed what the Fourteenth Amendment (and Reconstruction more generally) meant for African Americans. The Court said that the new amendments were supposed to guarantee "the freedom of the slave race, the security and firm establishment of that freedom, and the protection of the newly-made freeman and citizen from the oppressions of those who had formerly exercised unlimited dominion over him."[25] Extraordinary action was necessary because "it was said that their lives were at the mercy of bad men, either because the laws for their protection were insufficient or were not enforced."[26] Furthermore, "they were in all those States denied the right of suffrage. The laws were administered by the white man alone. It was urged that a race of men distinctively marked as was the negro, living in the midst of another and dominant race, could never be fully secured in their person and their property without the right of suffrage."[27] As for the Equal Protection Clause, the Justices said that "the existence of laws in the States where the newly emancipated negroes resided, which discriminated with gross injustice and hardship against them as a class, was the evil to be remedied by this clause, and by it such laws are forbidden."[28]

Of course, the Court gave none of these statements any content, because the butchers in *Slaughter-House* were white. But the flood of litigation that followed forced the Justices into a more searching inquiry on all three of the issues raised by that first Fourteenth Amendment case: property and contract rights, incorporation, and racial equality.

Stalemate in the Courts

Using the basic outline sketched out in *Slaughter-House*, lawyers pressed forward with a series of claims that attempted to put some meat on its bones. While some patterns emerged over the next two decades, there was no resolution of the main interpretive questions. Indeed, there were many inconsistent trends in the Fourteenth Amendment cases prior to the mid-1890s.

On the subject of *Slaughter-House*'s holding—whether the Fourteenth Amendment placed limits on state regulation of property and contracts—the Justices were steadfast in saying no. For example, the Court rejected a constitutional challenge to state grain-elevator rate ceilings in the 1870s, saying: "It was not supposed that statutes regulating the use, or even the price of the use, of private property necessarily deprived an owner of his property without due process of law."[29] A suit in the 1880s claiming that a state prohibition on liquor sales was unconstitutional was rejected on similar grounds, since "society has the power to protect itself, by legislation, from the injurious consequences of that business."[30] And when railroads attacked state rate regulations using the same Fourteenth Amendment theory, those challenges also failed.[31] Although the Court did hold out the prospect that a state law affecting economic rights could violate the Fourteenth Amendment under extreme conditions, it never invalidated a state statute for a substantive defect until 1894.[32]

At the same time, however, a countercurrent inside and outside the Court supported the nationalist reading of property and contract rights that was rejected in *Slaughter-House.* First, the dissenters in that case continued to criticize their brethren for leaving property rights at the mercy of grasping state legislatures, with Justice Bradley stating in one case that "the liberty of pursuit—the right to follow any of the ordinary callings of life— is one of the privileges of a citizen of the United States."[33] Next, some state courts adopted his logic when construing provisions in their state constitutions similar to the Fourteenth Amendment.[34] Finally, scholars such as Thomas M. Cooley provided intellectual support for protecting property and contract rights through constitutional law by drawing on antebellum suspicions of class legislation.[35] Thus, the debate over this aspect of *Slaughter-House* was not settled by the 1890s, even though critics of constitutional interference in state economic policy still narrowly held the upper hand.

On incorporation, the Court took a more nuanced approach: it rejected applying the procedures of the Bill of Rights (for example, grand jury, civil jury, and trial jury) to the states but expressed qualified support for extending its substantive provisions.[36] This distinction rested on the idea that procedures were only a means to achieving substantive justice and were subject to improvement, so fixing them in state law would retard progress.[37] For instance, when the Justices held in 1884 that the grand jury indictment rule of the Fifth Amendment did not apply to the states, they explained that fundamental rights were best "preserved and developed by a progressive growth and wise adaptation to new circumstances and situations of the forms and processes found fit to give, from time to time, new expression and greater effect to modern ideas of self-government."[38] Thus, the Constitution "must be held to guaranty, not particular forms of procedure, but the very substance of individual rights to life, liberty, and property."[39]

When those substantive claims came to the Court in an incorporation context, they received more favorable treatment.[40] For example, in *O'Neil v. Vermont* a defendant was convicted of selling liquor without a license and sentenced to fifty-four years in prison under a state statute that mandated extra jail time if a defendant could not pay the fines imposed.[41] The Court held that it could not consider whether this long sentence violated the Cruel and Unusual Punishments Clause of the Eighth Amendment, because the issue was not raised in O'Neil's brief.[42] But three Justices rejected this holding and, reaching the merits, held that the sentence was invalid.[43] Justice Field again led the charge, reasoning that the Fourteenth Amendment meant that when the

Bill of Rights declares or recognizes "the rights of persons they are rights belonging to them as citizens of the United States under the constitution . . . [and] no state shall make or enforce any law which shall abridge them."[44] From this principle, he deduced that "the state cannot apply . . . any more than the United States, the torture, the rack, or thumb-screw, or any cruel and unusual punishment, or any more than it deny . . . security in his house, papers, and effects against unreasonable searches and seizures."[45] Justice John Marshall Harlan, joined by Justice David Brewer, also dissented and explained that "since the adoption of the fourteenth amendment, no one of the fundamental rights of life, liberty, or property, recognized and guarantied by the constitution of the United States, can be denied or abridged by a state in respect to any person within its jurisdiction."[46]

As a result, the picture of incorporation at the start of the Populist period was less certain than is generally thought, in large part owing to the erroneous, though common, view that *Slaughter-House* resolved the issue. The idea that the entire Bill of Rights applied to the states was clearly rejected by the cases about jury rights. But this position was not tantamount to a conclusion that all of the parts of the first eight amendments were unincorporated. In fact, the opposite is true. The Justices supported extending the bill's substantive freedoms against state action when the issue was squarely presented to them. The problem, at least from the perspective of those in favor of that result, was that almost all of the cases following *Slaughter-House* concerned procedural rights rather than substantive ones.[47]

Racial classifications under the Fourteenth Amendment produced the widest split in the cases, with the Court seemingly unable to make up its mind between the egalitarian vision of Reconstruction and the traditional view of states' rights. On the positive side, the Justices struck down a West Virginia statute that barred African Americans from serving on criminal trial juries, stating that the new constitutional "design was to protect an emancipated race, and to strike down all possible legal discriminations against those who belong to it."[48] The Court also upheld the part of the Civil Rights Act of 1875 that banned racial discrimination in jury selection as a valid exercise of Congress's authority to enforce the Fourteenth Amendment.[49] And the Court expanded the Equal Protection Clause to include Asian Americans in a case involving a California law that was race-neutral on its face but was applied in a discriminatory manner against Chinese laundries; it stated that if a law "is applied and administered by the public authority with an evil eye and an unequal hand . . . the denial of equal justice is still within the prohibition of the constitution."[50]

Other rulings were not so friendly to minority rights and foreshadowed the cruelty of Jim Crow. For instance, the Court upheld an Alabama law that imposed harsher penalties for interracial than for intraracial adultery because the law treated members of both races equally when they engaged in a prohibited

Justice John Marshall Harlan,
a lone dissenter in many of the
great cases during the Populist era.
Library of Congress.

relationship.[51] The Justices also held that the Fourteenth Amendment did not reach private racial discrimination and read a federal statute that barred the use of force or intimidation to prevent citizens from exercising their national rights as requiring a racist intent—an interpretation that rendered that statute a dead letter by allowing defendants to make the argument that their motive for violence was something other than racism and force prosecutors to prove otherwise.[52] Most damaging of all were the *Civil Rights Cases,* in which the Court invalidated the sections of the Civil Rights Act of 1875 that barred racial discrimination in hotels, theaters, public transportation, and other facilities.[53] This opinion, which held that Congress had the power to remedy only discriminatory "state laws or state proceedings" rather than private conduct, was challenged in Justice Harlan's dissent because "citizenship in this country necessarily imports equality of civil rights among citizens of every race in the same state."[54] Harlan's expansive interpretation would not be the law of the land until Congress passed a new Civil Rights Act that was up-held by the Court in 1964.[55]

It would be misleading to suggest that these cases on racial matters were of equal importance, but we can say that there was a respectable body of support for a broad interpretation of the Fourteenth Amendment well after Reconstruction. This view was no less credible than the one held by the dissenters to *Slaughter-House*'s holding on property and contract rights, where the case law was even more hostile. Just as those critics drew on state courts and academics for support, so advocates of racial equality were sustained by public opinion in the North, where many states enacted their own versions of the provisions of the Civil Rights Act that were wiped out by the Supreme Court.[56] C. Vann Woodward, the greatest modern historian on the South and the first to recognize the significance of what happened in the 1890s, contended that the 1870s and 1880s were "a time of experiment, testing, and uncertainty—quite different from the time of repression and rigid uniformity that was to come toward the end of the century."[57] Woodward's contention, along with the divided doctrine on economic issues and incorporation, raises a fundamental interpretive question about late-nineteenth-century constitutionalism.

A Trend, a Mistake, or a Shock?

One way to explain what occurred at the turn of the twentieth century is that the trends in the post–*Slaughter-House* decisions continued until they reached their logical conclusion. For instance, *Maxwell*'s holding that no part of the Bill of Rights was a privilege or immunity of national citizenship followed from cases that made the same point with respect to rights like trial by civil jury. The decisions upholding Jim Crow, most notably the 1896 case of *Plessy v. Ferguson*, with its "separate but equal" rule validating racial segregation, can be seen as an extension of rulings, like the one in the *Civil Rights Cases*, that took a limited view of what racial equality meant.[58] Then there was *Lochner v. New York*, in which the Court held in 1905 that the Fourteenth Amendment protected a liberty of contract and barred the states from imposing unreasonable regulations (such as maximum hours or minimum wages).[59] This decision was consistent with the views of the *Slaughter-House* dissenters, which were gathering strength as the new century approached.

Another way to characterize these developments is that they were the product of negligent or malicious distortions that allowed the Supreme Court to impose its own preferences. On this reading, the liberty-of-contract doctrine was an illegitimate exercise of judicial power unmoored from the constitutional text, which is why the term "Lochnerizing" is still considered an insult.[60] For incorporation, the argument is that the Court took it upon itself to disregard the intent of the Framers of the Fourteenth Amendment because it thought that extending the Bill of Rights to the states would damage federalism.[61] Along the same lines, the validation of Jim Crow is sometimes described as an exercise in judicial sophistry, especially in *Plessy*'s statement that "the assumption that the enforced separation of the two races stamps the colored race with a badge of inferiority" was sound only if "the colored race chooses to put that construction upon it."[62]

Each of these schools of thought suffers from problems, but explaining why the "doctrinal trend" answer is unsatisfactory requires more effort than just pointing them out. For starters, some exceptions cannot be explained by the argument that the cases evolved in a consistent way after 1873. The Takings Clause, for example, was applied to the states during the 1890s.[63] Why was that clause set apart from the more general rejection of incorporation? Moreover, there was no trend toward holding state statutes regulating property and contract rights unconstitutional under the Fourteenth Amendment before the 1890s.[64] The Court's adoption of the liberty-of-contract doctrine in 1897—the same year that the Takings Clause was extended— effectively overturned *Slaughter-House* by holding that the Due Process Clause did guarantee the right "to pursue any livelihood or avocation."[65] That decision marked a sharp break with precedent, not a gradual adjustment, and aggressive behavior is evident in other decisions handed down at this time, as chapter 4 shows.[66]

Another problem with the argument that a trend in the cases explains how the Fourteenth Amendment looked by 1900 is that seeing a trend could be an example of "hindsight bias." This error "arises from an intuitive sense that the outcome that actually happened must have been inevitable. People allow their knowledge to influence their sense of what would have been predictable."[67] In other words, it is easy to say that the cases were moving in a certain direction when the final destination is known, and if they had ended up somewhere else, that would have looked natural, too. Hindsight bias is particularly important in analyzing the 1890s because, as the rest of my argument in this book shows, the participants in that debate certainly did not think that the outcomes were ordained by the Court's prior decisions.[68]

Scholars of race relations often invoke this inevitability theme and argue that Jim Crow and *Plessy* were simply the products of a racist society. Michael Klarman, a highly respected historian of civil rights, contends that "the *Plessy* Court's race decisions reflected, far more than they created, the regressive racial climate of the era" and that it is "unlikely that contrary rulings would have significantly alleviated the oppression of blacks."[69] Charles Lofgren, the author of a leading study on *Plessy*, observes that "the nation's press met the decision mainly with apathy," which proves, he says, that the case expressed a consensus on race in favor of white supremacy.[70] The premise behind these statements about segregation, though not always stated, is that racism was endemic throughout the South and reverted to the mean after the brief interlude of Reconstruction when the Union Army was in control. According to this view, the Court's retreat on its reading of equal rights just reflected the unwavering hostility of white southerners.

A major problem with this view is the assumption that the white South was monolithic and unchanging with respect to how African Americans should be treated. That assumption is simply not true, as Woodward explained nearly sixty years ago.[71] The Populists campaigning in the South shared an egalitarian vision of race relations and achieved some success with that message during the 1890s.[72] Once the southern Populists were defeated, things got worse for African Americans—a lot worse. As Woodward said, "I fondly believe that most of my critics now concede that toward the end of the century an escalation in white fanaticism resulted in a rigidity and universality of the enforcement of discriminatory law that was a sufficient change to mark a new era in race relations."[73] The terrible racial climate that Klarman and Lofgren describe was in place around 1900, but what if the Populists had won?[74] Unless this counterfactual is far-fetched, we cannot say with confidence that a trend in the decisions explains Jim Crow, because politics might have played a role in shaping the outcome.[75] Even if the probability of a Populist victory was low, it is also possible that the racial climate that sustained Jim Crow resulted in part from conservative resistance to the Populists, which would support a political explanation rather than a doctrinal one.

The flaws in the trend theory, though, pale in comparison to the problems with the contention that the Court engaged in a negligent or willful distortion of Reconstruction. If religion is the answer for what science cannot understand, and dark matter is what physicists use to explain what they do not know about the universe, then judicial error is the lawyers' excuse for incomprehensible issues.[76] Courts make mistakes, of course, but the argument that they were sloppy over a period of many years across many different areas of doctrine really is far-fetched. Often a claim of judicial error is nothing more than a placeholder for a statement that the interpretation of the Constitution has changed substantially without a constitutional amendment. A sea change did occur around 1900, but the source of the change is a mystery to most lawyers.

My answer, as should be clear by now, is that the backlash against the Populist movement shifted the baseline of analysis and reconciled the split within Fourteenth Amendment doctrine in a way that was contrary to the objectives of William Jennings Bryan and his followers. In other words, fear rather than logic tipped the balance in the courts—the fear of a revolt that rose from the heartland like a prairie fire and invoked the revolutionary successes of earlier generations.

TWO

The Rise of Populism

> We are engaged in just such a contest as every generation
> must pass through. In times of quiet, abuses spring up . . .
> The people suffer until suffering ceases to be a virtue; they
> are patient until patience is exhausted, and then they arouse
> themselves, take back the reins of government and put the
> government back upon its old foundation.
> —WILLIAM JENNINGS BRYAN

The most important question in constitutional theory is not how courts should interpret the text, which is the subject of many books far longer than this one, but why popular movements emerge to challenge the legal order and alter interpretive assumptions. In the 1890s the Populist Party launched one of these transformative efforts and adopted the rhetoric of Jacksonian Democracy in arguing that wealthy interests were abusing their power and threatening individual freedom.[1] Unlike their predecessors, though, the Populists argued that the government needed increased authority to counter the influence of business and that African Americans were an essential part of any reform coalition.[2] These political activists were following a model that I call the "generational cycle" that explains why and how Americans mobilize for constitutional change.

28

The Opening Phase of the Generational Cycle

Lawyers are well aware that powerful democratic forces, at what Bruce Ackerman terms "constitutional moments," periodically shake the foundations of the political system and forge new first principles.[3] They are also keenly interested in what these revolutionaries—the Founding Fathers, for example, or Reconstruction Republicans—were thinking about when they wrote the fundamental American legal texts. But when it comes to why these shocks occur and whether they are linked, the legal community basically shrugs its shoulders. In other words, these outbursts are treated as "black swans," which are highly improbable and appear randomly.[4] This assumption is false. There is, in fact, a deep pattern underlying these events that can tell us a great deal about how the Constitution is actually read.

Thomas Jefferson famously argued that the Constitution should be revised every nineteen years so that each generation could shape its own destiny, and this turned out to be a pretty good prediction of how the law evolves in practice.[5] An underappreciated fact about the U.S. political system is that, starting with the American Revolution in the 1770s, an "unpredictable" popular movement appears about every thirty years and realigns the electorate, as noted in the introduction.[6] Each of these seismic shifts in the party system (that is, in the voting patterns that determine which party will dominate a given era) leads to a substantial change in constitutional law, although this political force is not the only one that shapes how judges behave.[7] What stands out from this simple observation is that thirty years corresponds roughly to the lifespan of a generation. The passage of time, therefore, seems to provide a crucial diagnostic for why and when legal change occurs.

Attorneys are trained to think in linear terms—a line of cases—and thus the notion of a constitutional cycle may seem strange, but in other disciplines the idea that human psychology leads to repetitive behavior is widely accepted. Economics has the business cycle with its bubbles and busts, although that runs on a tighter schedule than once every thirty years.[8] Thomas Kuhn showed that science follows a similar path, albeit within a much longer time frame, as each field periodically finds itself in the thrall of a theory articulated by a leader (Aristotle, Newton, Einstein) until that approach is no longer able to explain observable data and is replaced by a new paradigm.[9] Furthermore, social practices ranging from fashion to baby names move in cycles, so why should constitutional law be any different?[10] The answer is that constitutional law is not any different.

The explanation for the temporal pattern in law comes from research demonstrating that people within a similar age-group—a generational cohort—tend to vote in a similar way because they are buffeted by a common set of events.[11] This makes sense for at least three reasons. First, as the "availability heuristic" tells us in this context, living through an event has a much greater impact than studying it, especially since history can so easily be dismissed as ancient.[12] Second, most people form their political attitudes (along with their taste in music) when they are young, and tend to stick to them throughout their lives. Third, only one generation can come of age and experience a particular event in a visceral way—a crisis like World War II or the terrorist attacks of September 11, 2001. These tendencies result in a stable set of political preferences that emerge around each generational cohort. Once the dust settles from whatever crises prove decisive, the party that crystallizes the majority view of what just happened becomes the leading national political force. That party then retains power over the next several elections by reminding voters of the abuses that caused them to swear allegiance or switch it. For instance, after the Civil War, Republicans maintained their control by "waving the bloody shirt" and using the Democrats' support for secession as a reason to deem them unfit for office. Since turnabout is fair play, long after the Depression, Democrats ran against Herbert Hoover and the fear that Republican rule would bring back breadlines. In both cases, these campaign themes stood for a broader constitutional ideology that was the dominant ethos during those periods.

The same temporal forces that create generational cohorts and sustain their respective majority parties eventually undermine both. As time marches on, the membership of the generation with firsthand knowledge of the relevant events diminishes: people die. Meanwhile, new voters enter the system and pass through other storms that lead them to form their own conclusions and to discount claims about treason or bread lines as mere rhetoric. The key question is, When does the latter group outnumber the former and create a political tipping point? Viewed in this light, the frequency of electoral realignments is not arbitrary: thirty years is about how long it takes for one generational cohort to be supplanted by another.

Nevertheless, this constitutional cycle involves more than mere head counting, for a lengthy period of one-party control also makes it more likely that abuses will mount and cause voters to reconsider their loyalties. In part, this is because corruption and complacency are the inevitable symptoms of a lengthy incumbency. A political movement also tends to keep extending its core principles (through inertia if nothing else) as long as it holds on to power, and the momentum eventually takes the principles too far for some faction that changes sides and gives the other party a majority—the Reagan Democrats are a recent example. Going too far is just shorthand to describe ideas that were designed to solve a set of concrete problems decades earlier but are now exacerbating the current malaise, from rising sectional divisions during the 1850s to the Panic of 2008. At that point, the political arena is ripe for a surge of activism that establishes a new generational cohort and starts the cycle again.

Viewing constitutional law from a generational perspective yields many fruitful insights, since the process repeats itself often and presents analogies between events from different eras that occurred at a similar point within their respective generations.

The particulars of that approach are discussed throughout this book, but there are three clear lessons about how these popular movements get started. First, sweeping change typically begins with a tiny band of radicals who take advantage of the natural decay in the political order. Second, the seeds of a new generation are sown when its predecessor first assumes power—as was the case for the revival of abolitionism caused by Andrew Jackson's brutal removal of the Cherokees along the Trail of Tears during the 1830s.[13] As Walter Bagehot, an English journalist and constitutional analyst, once explained: "A political country is like an American forest; you have only to cut down the old trees, and immediately new trees come up to replace them; the seeds were waiting in the ground, and they began to grow as soon as the withdrawal of the old ones brought in light and air."[14] Third, each new movement is defined by the wrongs that it seeks to correct, and it must turn to novel constitutional theories to provide the necessary remedies.

Discontent at the Grass Roots

The creation myth of the Populists dates back to 1873, the year in which *Slaughter-House* was decided by the Republican generation. Congress enacted the Coinage Act, which established the gold standard: silver would no longer be part of the money supply.[15] The act attracted virtually no attention because very few silver dollars were being minted, though a few

33

people did complain that demonetizing silver would harm debtors by creating a tight monetary policy. But twenty years later this decision was widely known as the Crime of '73, part of a fiendish plot by bankers and industrialists to impoverish the people through deflation.[16] The hardy group of agrarian dissenters that made this claim was the nucleus of the Populist movement.

The paranoia about the Crime of '73 was indicative of a broader feeling among farmers that their status was in decline because of forces beyond their control. In 1893, Frederick Jackson Turner advanced his influential thesis that the frontier was a key part of American culture and that its disappearance had profound consequences.[17] Although his particular view has been challenged, the lost frontier metaphor captured the reality that rural culture was going through a wrenching transition caused by the Industrial Revolution. Innovations in technology raised the productivity of agriculture and linked regional markets into a global one. Increases in production led to a sustained deflation in prices, which made it more difficult for farmers to obtain credit. Often the only way to survive was by mortgaging part of a current crop to buy seed and equipment for the next year. This crop-lien plan just deepened the debt cycle.[18]

Mounting debts were not the only problem facing farmers, for they also found their lives increasingly dictated by corporate interests. The independent yeoman of old now was dependent on banks for loans, grain elevators for storing crops, and railroads for bringing his goods to market. Regulation of the financial, storage, and transportation industries was weak, and those businesses held a major bargaining advantage, so all of them could charge discriminatory rates.[19] Rural voters also thought that the trusts now had a stranglehold on government and were using that power to turn farmers into serfs.[20] Thomas E. Watson, a young lawyer from Georgia who became the Populist Party's leader in the South, expressed these fears in vivid language:

> These corporations are the Feudal Barons of this Century. Their Directors live in lordly Palaces and Castles . . . They keep bands of Militia to do their fighting . . . At the word of command these hireling assassins shoot down men, women, and children . . .
>
> Not only do the corporations keep armed Retainers: they keep Oily and servile Courtiers to do their bidding in other walks of life. Their paid Lobby bribes the voter. Their paid editor feeds the public with lies. Their corrupt Lawyers and Judges peddle out justice to the highest bidder. Their Attorneys go on the Bench or into Senates to vote the will of their Masters.[21]

The omnipresent corporate power that Watson described was especially galling to those in rural communities, who adhered to the Jeffersonian ideal that they were the heart of the republic and that liberty could not endure in a commercial world.

Driven by these economic concerns, agrarian interests tried to organize through the Grange Movement and the Greenback Party, but their efforts came to naught until the formation of the Farmers' Alliance in the 1880s.[22] This umbrella organization, which was the forerunner of the Populist Party, avoided politics and stressed the need for farmers to join together to enhance their leverage.[23] That appeal for collective action struck a chord: more than three million people flocked to the alliance banner.[24] A sympathetic newspaper explained that the "people are aroused at last. Never in our history has there been such a union of action among farmers as now."[25] Despite this impressive result, alliance leaders soon realized that self-help would not be enough. They needed to enter the political arena and bring the power of government to bear on their problems.[26]

To see why agrarian activists made the expansion of federal authority a central part of their ideology, consider the silver issue raised by the Crime of '73.[27] Most farmers rejected the argument that deflation in commodity prices was the result of technology or globalization. Instead, they blamed the gold standard. That was the basis for Bryan's legendary vow in the 1896 campaign: "you shall not crucify mankind upon a cross of gold."[28] Senator William Allen of Kansas explained the results of that policy as "the operation of a shrinking volume of money . . . [by which] the East has placed its hands on the throat of the West."[29] When the Farmers' Alliance held its first national congress in 1889, the platform called for both the issuance of legal tender "in sufficient volume to do the business of the country on a cash system" and "the free and unlimited coinage of silver."[30] In both of these planks, agrarian activists were acknowledging that only federal action could address their plight.

Enthusiasm for public intervention and collective action was also on display in the alliance's position on the best way to deal with railroads and other industries: for the government to own and operate them.[31] The most popular novel of the day, *Looking Backward*, set in the year 2000, described a utopia based on nationalizing the means of production.[32] Although nationalization would give federal bureaucrats unprecedented power over the economy, reformers argued that "where a business is so clearly of a public nature that the individual can only get fair treatment by having the government to act for all, then individualism ceases to be wise and nationalism becomes . . . necessary."[33] The contours of this idea were never fully explored, but the Populists eventually called for a takeover of the railroads, the telegraph, the telephone network, and banks.[34]

These proposals reflected a broad constitutional judgment that the industrial age required government to secure positive rights and redistribute income. Ignatius Donnelly, a leading drafter of the Populist Party platform, dismissed the idea that freedom consisted only of a lack of restraints imposed by the state. He wondered: "What is freedom worth to a man who is dying of hunger? . . . Can you keep a room warm, next winter, with the thermometer at 30° below zero, by reciting the Declaration of Independence?"[35] Spurred by this belief in affirmative liberty, the Populists also made a progressive income tax a key goal and demanded the phase-out of corporate subsidies. Together, these actions would, they argued, prevent the governmental injustice that bred the "two great classes—tramps and millionaires."[36]

In addition to these bread-and-butter reforms, the agrarian movement sought to curb the influence of the "Money Power" by backing a series of structural changes that would promote direct democracy. For example, Populists supported the use of secret ballots to reduce vote fraud; state initiatives and referenda to bypass corrupt state legislatures; and the election of senators by popular vote.[37] Other reforms backed by rural strategists were women's suffrage, the abolition of the Electoral College, and the eight-hour workday.[38] Through these changes, the Populists vowed to "restore the government of the Republic to the hands of 'the plain people,' with whose class it originated."[39]

Other parts of the agrarian agenda had a distinctly illiberal cast—most notably, nativism. In a sense, the Populists were the last hurrah of the Anglo-Saxon Protestant population that made up the core of the constitutional generations led by Jefferson, Jackson, and Lincoln. The party not only opposed alien ownership of land but rejected opening "our ports to the pauper and criminal classes of the world" and demanded the "further restriction of undesirable immigration."[40] Tom Watson, for all of his reforming zeal, was also convinced that the "scum of creation has been dumped on us. Some of our principal cities are more foreign than American . . . The vice and crime which they have planted in our midst are sickening and terrifying."[41] This hostility to foreigners crippled Bryan when he ran for president because the urban voters that he needed were largely recent immigrants. And their suspicion of the Populists was compounded by the fact that the agrarian movement was mostly Protestant while the cities were mostly Catholic, and there was no love lost between these denominations in the nineteenth century.

In 1891, after a series of meetings across the Midwest, the Farmers' Alliance and other like-minded groups formed the People's Party. We may think it odd that reformers would form a new party rather than seize control of one of the two major parties, but the example that was in their minds was the Republican revolution of the 1850s, in which antislavery activists repudiated the Whigs and decided to start a new party from scratch. Indeed, the Populists often invoked the struggle against slavery as a model, even paraphrasing the Supreme Court's line in *Dred Scott v. Sandford* that African Americans had no rights that whites were bound to respect: "The oppressed of to-day are white laborers and mechanics who, evidently, though without a Supreme Court decision, have no rights which millionaires and moneyed corporations are bound to respect."[42] The party nominated James B. Weaver, a former Union general and agrarian organizer, as its first presidential candidate in 1892, and his constitutional views are worth exploring in some depth.[43]

Populism and the Commerce Clause

The history of the rural revolt during the 1890s is well known, but the creativity of Populist lawyers is often overlooked. Given the party's ambitious agenda, its leaders needed some new interpretive concepts to support their policies. On some issues, such as ending the gold standard and introducing a progressive income tax, the cases supported (or so it seemed) the power of Congress to act.[44] For other items, especially nationalization, leaders like Weaver and Marion Butler, the Populist chief in North Carolina, looked to the Commerce Clause for support.[45] The fog of time obscures just how innovative this tactic was and diminishes what was the most lasting contribution of Populism.

Weaver framed his campaign in a book entitled *A Call to Action* that laid out the Populist platform and presented a legal analysis of the party's goals. Starting as Lincoln did, with the Declaration of Independence, Weaver asked if it could "be denied that all men have a natural right to a portion of the soil" as part of their inalienable rights.[46] His conclusion was that this right was "as sacred as their right to life itself" and that "these propositions are so manifestly true as to lie beyond the domain of controversy."[47] The problem was that these rights could not be exercised without ready access to credit and transportation, which "are the instrumentalities through which the natural rights of man are rendered available in organized society."[48] Weaver was therefore troubled by some recent cases holding that

James B. Weaver, the
Populist Party's presi-
dential nominee in 1892.
Library of Congress.

the Dormant Commerce Clause barred the states from regulating liquor and railroad traffic that crossed their borders.

Weaver found the present state of affairs inconsistent with first principles. The Framers recognized that the natural right to the soil was inseparable from the control of credit and transportation, which, he said, was why they incorporated the Commerce Clause "among other far-reaching and sweeping provisions" in the Constitution.[50] He added that "whatever may be the meaning of this provision, it is certain that the framers . . . regarded the power to be exercised as too important to be confided to the discretion of individuals or left to the control of the States."[51] Similarly, Marion Butler said that the Commerce Clause should

Marion Butler, the Populist
senator from North Carolina.
Library of Congress.

be reinterpreted in broad terms owing to "the greatest social,
industrial and political evolution the world has ever seen."[52] In
Weaver's eyes, Congress was ignoring its obligations by dele-
gating its commerce power to the trusts and allowing them to
"crush out the inalienable rights of the people."[53] He went on to
specify the "great object of the Industrial movement now challenging public attention," which was "to restore to Congress
its Constitutional and exclusive control over the great limbs of
commerce, money, transportation and telegraphy."[54]

This line of reasoning was groundbreaking at the time because nobody else viewed the Commerce Clause in such sweeping terms. Most lawyers know that Chief Justice John Marshall
interpreted the clause for the first time in *Gibbons v. Ogden.*[55]
Until 1895, however, the Court largely ignored this provision.

None of the great nineteenth-century cases on congressional authority—*M'Culloch v. Maryland, Dred Scott*, the *Legal Tender Cases*, the *Trade-Mark Cases*, or the *Civil Rights Cases*—focused on the Commerce Clause.[56] To the extent that the Justices made strong assertions of national power, they relied on other textual provisions or on a general claim that Congress could act under its implied authority.

Although the scope of the commerce power started expanding with the creation of the Interstate Commerce Commission in 1887 and passage of the Sherman Antitrust Act in 1890, these developments were tentative.[57] When Senator John Sherman of Ohio introduced his bill, he denied that the commerce power was applicable. His position was that the only constitutional way to regulate trusts was with punitive taxes.[58] The Farmers' Alliance, which was the backbone of the Populist movement, lobbied for a broader approach, and Congress came around to the view that the Commerce Clause could sustain federal regulation.[59] Thus, from its very inception, the idea of reading the Commerce Clause expansively was tied to the agrarian agenda. The Supreme Court would soon be forced to engage these arguments, although its approach would be rather different from Weaver's.

The Populists get no credit for catapulting the Commerce Clause into legal orthodoxy because most people think that John Marshall did all of the work in *Gibbons*. There was some expansive language in that decision, but hardly anyone took those statements seriously until a popular movement came along that took a similar position.[60] The same was true for his opinion in *M'Culloch*, which was basically ignored until Reconstruction, when Republicans revived the case in an effort to elaborate a more nationalist vision in the wake of the Civil War.[61] As we shall see in chapter 4, *Marbury* went through the same rediscovery process when conservatives wanted to use that case to turn back the Populist wave.

Southern Populism and Race

Southern Populists shared the economic and political goals of the national movement, but they took a much greater interest in addressing racial inequality because they needed African American votes to win at the state level. These party leaders were not Lyndon B. Johnson or Jimmy Carter—they still believed in white supremacy.[62] In the South, Populists could overcome the Democratic advantage only by forming a class alliance with black sharecroppers (and the few Republicans that remained). The immediate political needs of the rising constitutional generation prompted their embrace of radical ideas, just as it motivated their embrace of the Commerce Clause: "self interest always controls," as Tom Watson explained.[63] Of course, the electoral universe in which the Populists operated was shaped by the Fifteenth Amendment's grant of the vote to the freed slaves, and that vote was still large enough in the early 1890s to attract politicians.[64]

The result was the most egalitarian movement within the South until the late twentieth century, one that stressed the protection of African American rights and the need for joint action on economic affairs.[65] For example, the Populists went to great lengths to create a diverse (at least by the standards of the day) alliance. Henry Demarest Lloyd, a noted Populist writer, said the party gave the "negroes of the South a political fellowship which they have never obtained, not even from their saviors, the Republicans"; African Americans were even appointed to significant committees.[66] Furthermore, agrarian activists took a strong stand against lynching, for the right to vote, and for the right to serve on juries. The Georgia Populist platform stated, "We condemn lynching and demand of our public servants the rigid enforcement of our laws against this barbarous practice," and some party members backed that position by using force to stop white mobs intent on lynching.[67] As an Alabama party official said, "The negroes well know that it is to the People's Party of Alabama that they must look for the continued enjoyment of those rights guarantied to them by the constitution."[68]

On the stump, Populist candidates asked for African American support in language that was not heard again in the South until the enactment of the Voting Rights Act in 1965. Watson told voters in 1892 that only a union of farmers across racial lines could bring about real change: "You are kept apart that you may be separately fleeced of your earnings. You are made to hate each other because upon that hatred is rested the keystone of the arch of financial despotism which enslaves you both. You are deceived and blinded that you may not see how this race antagonism perpetuates a monetary system which beggars both."[69] This plea for unity was reinforced by having white and African American candidates campaign together and by issuing appeals tailored to black sharecroppers. A letter to the editor from an African American voter that appeared in a Populist paper (and may have been planted) stated that the "fact that the Populist party has the courage of its convictions to denounce the lynching spirit in the State is commendable and deserving of the sympathy and support of our people . . . who will be the greatest beneficiaries if lynch law is checked."[70] The writer added that Populists were working "for a free ballot and a fair count, and pledging the enactment of laws securing this to every legal voter," for "no one more than negroes have suffered under the suppression of the ballot."[71]

While the Populists worked to transcend racial distinctions in the South, sectional divisions still plagued the party. In the rest of the country, agrarian reformers aligned themselves with Democrats, their natural coalition partners against Republicans, who were more supportive of manufacturing and financial interests. Indeed, this was the "fusion" that Bryan completed in 1896, when he was the Populist and Democratic presidential candidate. Down South, the alliance was reversed because of Reconstruction's legacy. Democrats were the common enemy of Republicans and Populists alike. The party tried to finesse the regional schism by giving Weaver, with his Union army service, an ex-Confederate running mate, but this ticket did not prevent Weaver from having to dodge a barrage of rotten eggs when he campaigned in Georgia.[72] This structural flaw in Populism also explains why the national organization, including Bryan himself, took no interest in racial matters.[73] Activists in Nebraska did not need African American votes to enact their economic agenda, so they just did not care what happened to the former slaves.

Nevertheless, Weaver won more than a million votes and carried five states in 1892.[74] The down-ticket results were also encouraging, for Populist governors won in three states and other party members swept into Congress.[75] Even though the actual winners of the election were Grover Cleveland and the Democrats, there was a sense that Populists were on the cusp of a breakthrough. As one pamphleteer stated, "A party which comes into existence in the summer and polls considerably over a million votes in the fall cannot be ignored much longer."[76] And "if things go on as they are going now, at the next presidential election the golden calf will be ground to powder, and the people will—for the first time since the war—rule for themselves. But the Wall street men will make a terrible fight . . . every possible trick and misrepresentation will be tried to set the people on a false scent."[77]

THREE

Resistance North and South

Those who disregard this warning and persist in taking part
with a riotous mob in forcibly resisting and obstructing the
execution of the laws of the United States . . . can not be
regarded otherwise than as public enemies.
—GROVER CLEVELAND

Reform leads to resistance, and resistance leads to reform. This
feedback loop propels each turn of the generational cycle, for the
new popular movement inevitably faces opposition from a prior
one that holds the reins of power. That obstacle causes reformers to escalate their demands and triggers a process of "mutual
transformation" in which the electorate becomes polarized.[1] In
the 1890s the leader of the conservative backlash against the
Populists was Grover Cleveland, and his role in the drama that
unfolded was crucial. With the onset of the Panic of 1893, during which unemployment skyrocketed to unprecedented levels,
anger at Cleveland's policies exploded in a series of protests that
challenged elite attitudes toward property rights and federalism.[2]
In the South, the fight against the Populists was a factor in the
passage of the first Jim Crow laws, which segregated railroads.

All of these challenges and reactions highlight a basic paradox of constitutional resistance: defending the status quo ends up dramatically changing the law.[3]

The Second Phase of the Generational Cycle

Although there are many heroic examples of citizens who fought radical changes to American legal traditions, the foes of the broad popular uprisings that define constitutional generations are generally viewed negatively. The reason is simple: they lost, and in the process the voters rejected their values and endorsed a totally different approach.[4] But during the 1890s the result was more ambiguous, as Bryan's reputation remains dismal even though his critics supported doctrines that are now discredited. Before exploring why the taint remains, we should understand the dynamic that is created when, as Senator Thomas Hart Benton said in the 1850s, constitutional generations collide and "old light shining steadily in a calm atmosphere" must engage "a new light, suddenly breaking out, and flashing fitfully in the bursts of a raging tempest."[5]

One way of thinking about what happens during a popular debate over constitutional principles comes from the work of Reva Siegel, who argues that in the search for support from the median voter, each side moderates its demands, and their positions converge.[6] She points to the ratification struggle over the Equal Rights Amendment in the 1970s, in which supporters of the proposal were forced to disavow the claim that the amendment would mandate abortion rights or legalize same-sex marriage, while foes of the amendment had to concede that some forms of gender discrimination were unconstitutional under the Fourteenth Amendment.[7] This example, in her view, shows that "counter movements can discipline an insurgency's transformative claims on the Constitution so that proposed understandings ultimately assume a form in which they can be integrated into the tradition they challenge."[8] One result of this process is that "each movement is forced to take account of the other's arguments, and in time may even begin to incorporate aspects of the other's arguments into its own claims."[9]

Parts of Siegel's analysis are helpful for understanding the generational cycle, but the clashes that lead to an electoral realignment show a pronounced tendency to escalate (both in their objectives and in their tactics) rather than to moderate.[10] In this respect, the most helpful analogy comes from the Prussian war theorist Carl von Clausewitz. His dictum that "war is nothing but the continuation of policy with other means" can be turned around to show that constitutional politics and war have a lot in common.[11] Both are conducted in an atmosphere of high uncertainty, and a basic tension exists between the rational objectives being pursued and the passions stirred up among (and needed to motivate) the people fighting for those goals. Clausewitz said it was a "fallacy to imagine war between civilized peoples as resulting merely from a rational act on the part of their governments and to conceive of war as gradually ridding itself of passion." According to him, the passion of warfare polarizes the parties in conflict and mutually transforms them. In other words, an act by one side "compels its opponent to follow suit; a reciprocal action is started which must lead, in theory, to extremes." This instinct to respond with greater strength rests on uncertainty about the outcome, because "so long as I have not overthrown my opponent I am bound to fear he may overthrow me. Thus I am not in control: he dictates to me as much as I dictate to him."[12] The cycle of escalation ends only when one side is overwhelmed or capitulates.

Anger or passion about ongoing abuses is the emotion that motivates those mobilizing for change, but fear is the driving force for constitutional conservatives. To borrow another thought from Clausewitz, in war and politics people overstate the consequences of defeat because of their uncertainty and fill "the stage with scenery crudely daubed with fearsome apparitions."[13] Even the soberest lawyers hit the panic button when their principles fall under attack by a popular movement.[14] Indeed, the generational cycle is replete with examples of officials concluding that unusual steps must be taken to save the Constitution from destruction, even if that means striking against the insurgents before they assume power. Such preemptive actions against change are why resistance warps the law. Since the main goal of the opposition is to discredit reform, conservatives are often presented with a choice between applying precedent honestly (even if that means letting their enemies obtain a political victory) or recasting the law to ensure that reformers lose. The question of how best to respond has no consistent answer, but in many instances the fear of defeat outweighs respect for the rules.[15] None of this suggests that the behavior of conservatives, in the 1890s or at any other time, is unhealthy. One person's polarized debate is another's vigorous discussion.[16] An intense contest can also be a stimulus for creativity, as shown by the Populists' rediscovery of the Commerce Clause.

One final point must be made about the resistance mounted during the 1890s, and it is that conservatives who represented the Reconstruction generation painted the Populists with a broad and indiscriminate brush. In other words, they tended to lump agrarian reformers with labor activists as "revolutionaries" who had to be stopped, even though these groups often had little in common except animus toward President Cleveland. Thus, the use of the term "Populists" in the press or by some politicians was not always accurate. Still, the backlash against reformers was genuine whether it was directed at the real Populists or at others. So let us plunge into the maelstrom created by the Panic of 1893 and revisit what one historian calls "the *année terrible* of American history between Reconstruction and the [First] World War."[17]

Grover Cleveland and the Pullman Strike

The emergency created by the panic, which came on the heels of President Cleveland's narrow victory in 1892, gave him a terrific

President Grover Cleveland.
Library of Congress.

opportunity to expand his coalition. By embracing some Populist proposals and offering help to dispossessed farmers and workers, he could have neutralized the new third party while putting the Republicans in the difficult position of opposing these relief measures. Indeed, Franklin D. Roosevelt used a similar strategy in the 1930s to build the New Deal majority. Cleveland was a skilled politician capable of pulling off such a maneuver—he was, after all, the only Democrat to win the presidency between 1860 and 1912. The problem was that he represented the faction of the party that backed the gold standard and was deeply skeptical of state intervention in the economy, which had been the political consensus since Reconstruction.[18] In 1893, Cleveland faced his first moment of truth. Should he limit the damage to his principles by joining the popular movement or stand fast and risk defeat?

Cleveland did extend one modest olive branch, but on every other issue he was in a fighting mood. When Congress passed an income tax co-sponsored by a young representative from Nebraska named William Jennings Bryan, he allowed the bill to become law without his signature.[19] This action (or, more precisely, lack of action) was taken because the revenue from the tax allowed for lower tariffs, which was one of the president's priorities. When it came to monetary policy, however, Cleveland rejected any compromise with the Populists. He blamed the panic on an 1890 law that ordered the Treasury to buy silver and then issue notes against those purchases to placate the demand for unlimited silver coinage.[20] Claiming that this policy undermined confidence in the banking system, Cleveland convened a special session of Congress and rammed through a repeal of the silver statute.[21] He stuck to a firm gold standard after that, and when the Treasury's gold reserves dropped dangerously low in 1895, he even called upon J. P. Morgan to form a syndicate that would sell bonds in order to buy more gold.[22] In those days, Wall Street bailed out the government instead of the other way around.

These actions by the president marked the first escalation of the fight between the Populists and the political establishment. Although Marion Butler lambasted Cleveland as a "tool of corporate interest, a traitor, and a drunkard," other agrarian activists took a more sanguine view.[23] Tom Watson declared that the new administration was "a God-send to us" because it would bring conservative attitudes "into the clear light, where all honest citizens can see."[24] He predicted that Cleveland's policies would lead to more polarization, which could only redound to the benefit of the Populists, for "Democrats who hold Republican doctrines will be driven to the Republican Party, and vice versa. Members of the two old parties who really hold Populist views, finding no support in either Democratic or Republican ranks, will be driven to the People's Party."[25] Watson's comments neatly summarize the mutual transformation that occurs during a clash between rival generations. By taking stern action to snuff out a new constitutional movement, Cleveland ended up intensifying both the Populists' support and their demands.

Agrarian leaders responded to Cleveland's unbending stance with a campaign of protests and civil disobedience. In the spring of 1894 a party activist from Ohio, Jacob Coxey, led a march of the unemployed to demand an extensive public works program. As "Coxey's Army" converged on Washington, D.C., the *New York Times* saw a "Battle between Law and Anarchy," and federal officials rushed troops into the city.[26] When the "petition in boots" reached the capital, the police welcomed the marchers with beatings and arrests. Demonstrations and sympathy strikes soon broke out in other cities: "in no civilized country in this century, not actually in the throes of war or open insurrection, has society been so disorganized as it was in the United States during the first half of 1894."[27]

Without a doubt, the most important clash between reformers and the president came that summer with the Pullman Strike. The national work stoppage and the violence that followed it led to *In re Debs*, a major Supreme Court case on the Commerce Clause that is discussed in chapter 4.[28] Though the strike involved organized labor rather than the Populists, the reaction to what occurred is one of the more important—and yet underrated—legal events of the nineteenth century. The shock of that chaos created momentum for federal protection of property and contract rights and cooled enthusiasm for extending other essential liberties to the dissenters—rural and urban—who were in the streets. Plenty of other strikes took place as the nascent labor movement, especially the Knights of Labor, sought to make its voice heard, but none of them penetrated the public consciousness like the Pullman Strike or had a greater impact on the Constitution.

The strike grew out of a dispute between Pullman, the leading producer of railroad cars, and the American Railway Union, led by Eugene V. Debs.[29] Most of the firm's work occurred in a company town near Chicago where workers paid rent to Pullman and bought supplies from company stores. After the panic, the firm slashed wages by more than 25 percent but refused to reduce rents and prices for employees, who had nowhere else to live. When the workers complained, their ringleaders were fired. This led to a strike that caught the attention of Debs, who called Pullman's concern for its workers "the same as the interest of a slave holder in his human chattels."[30] When Pullman rejected a

Eugene V. Debs, leader of
the Pullman Strike. Library
of Congress.

suggestion that the strike be resolved through arbitration, the national union called for a boycott of Pullman vehicles, which transformed the local dispute into a crisis by bringing railroad traffic to a halt across the nation.[31] *Harper's Weekly* wrote, with only slight overstatement, that America was paralyzed and "fighting for its own existence just as truly as in suppressing the great rebellion."[32]

This latest escalation of the constitutional confrontation created a legal minefield for the president. The railroad barons demanded an end to "blackmail" and wanted federal troops sent into Chicago "because that was the center and headquarters of the strike," and "*if smashed there*, it would collapse everywhere else."[33] But the governor of Illinois, John Peter Altgeld, supported the strike and opposed federal intervention.[34] He insisted that the federal government had no power to enter a sovereign state and interfere in its domestic affairs without its consent. So the president was faced with the argument that federalism, his party's touchstone for nearly a century, protected Debs and his colleagues. Cleveland was now forced to make another hard choice that all conservatives in the throes of constitutional resistance face. When the application of their principles would help their foes, what should they do?[35]

The U.S. attorney general, Richard Olney, answered that question by ignoring federalism and asserting that the Commerce Clause gave Cleveland the power to intervene. His tactic is a great example of Siegel's point that the opposing sides in a constitutional debate are compelled to respond to the other's arguments and try to turn them to their advantage. Whereas the Populists saw the Commerce Clause as a tool to create a level playing field for farmers, Olney saw it as an instrument to discipline unions. He argued that the strike disrupted mail deliveries, even though Debs pledged to exempt mail from the strike. Railroad owners, however, prevented the mail trains from moving and gave the administration the excuse it needed to get an injunction ordering the union to cease its strike.[36] When Debs refused to comply, Cleveland ordered in troops to break the strike and issued a decree stating that "it has become impracticable in the judgment of the President to enforce by the ordinary course of judicial proceedings, the laws of the United States within the State of Illinois, and especially in the city of Chicago."[37]

As workers and soldiers clashed throughout the city, Altgeld telegrammed the president demanding an end to the invasion. The governor held that "local self government is a fundamental principle of our constitution . . . Especially is this so in matters relating to the exercise of the police power and the preservation of law and order. To absolutely ignore a local government in matters of this kind . . . not only insults the people of this state . . . but is in violation of a basic principle of our institutions." Consistent with this defense of federalism, Altgeld denied that the federal government could send troops into Illinois unless he requested assistance. He argued that "the question of federal supremacy is in no way involved; . . . under our constitution federal supremacy and local self government must go hand in hand and to ignore the latter is to do violence to the constitution."[38]

The president answered Altgeld's protest with a brief telegram defending his actions. He said that the "post office department" had requested that "obstructions of the mails should be removed," so "federal troops were sent to Chicago in strict accordance with the constitutions and laws of the United States." Cleveland added that his decision was based upon "abundant proof that conspiracies existed against commerce between the states." Voices in the press backed his position, labeling Governor Altgeld a "sympathizer with riot, with violence, with lawlessness and with anarchy."[39] Critics who supported the strike responded: "From the White House down it has been determined to put forth every effort even to Gattling guns . . . to destroy this strike and the laboring people."[40]

Although the legality of Cleveland's action would be tested in the courts, it is worth pausing to consider how the strike influenced the contemporary debate on constitutional law. The first point that stands out is that both sides in this struggle focused on the Commerce Clause. It was in 1894 that the modern understanding of the commerce power as the wellspring of federal authority was established, even though there was no agreement on the purpose that this power was supposed to serve. The dialogue demonstrates the dynamic quality of constitutional discourse: each camp sought to overthrow the other through mutually escalating actions, but in the process they managed to construct a common interpretive principle.

A subtler feature of the Pullman Strike, exemplified by the Cleveland-Altgeld correspondence, was its impact on federalism. Contemporary observers were struck by the thought that the fight between the governor and the president was the most serious challenge to federal authority since the Civil War.[41] For the Populists, state governments were now the only remaining bulwark "against a threatened military government of the railroads and their associate monopolies."[42] Indeed, in his 1896 party platform Bryan made a full-throated defense of states' rights on this issue: "We denounce arbitrary interference by Federal authorities in local affairs as a violation of the Constitution of the United States and a crime against free institutions, and we especially object to government by injunction as a new and highly dangerous form of oppression by which Federal judges, in contempt of the laws of the States and rights of citizens, become at once legislators, judges, and executioners."[43] While Populists were enthusiastic about federal authority if that meant helping farmers, they argued that the president's view of the commerce power was contrary to the Guarantee Clause of the Constitution, which secures "to every State in this Union a Republican Form of Government, and shall protect each of them against Invasion; and on Application of the Legislature, or of the Executive (when the Legislature cannot be convened) against domestic Violence."[44] In Bryan's view, that text embodied the principle that local officials are "better qualified than the President to judge of the necessity for federal assistance" with respect to law-and-order issues.[45]

Conservatives replied that Bryan's insistence on resisting federal intervention was nothing more than an invitation to anarchy and that Cleveland's actions were necessary to protect property from a local mob. One Republican pamphlet said the Populists wanted to take "us back to 1861, when governors were abetting rebellion . . . This country is not ripe for such another struggle, nor ready to approve the doctrine that the Federal Government cannot fight for its own life in spite of all the mayors, governors, or sheriffs."[46] Cleveland's supporters pointed out that "the great Chicago railroad strike of 1894 was anything but a 'local affair.' It involved the railroad employees of fifteen states and was, incidentally, the cause of violence and rioting which almost amounted to open insurrection."[47] The attorney general added that federalism was "a far more serious matter than the money question, or any of the other questions now before the people, grave as they all are." If Populists would "do nothing to protect the property . . . of the United States unless and until the officers of another government request or consent, then we really have no Federal Government."

This fascinating back-and-forth indicates that the searing experience of the Pullman Strike started to change the way elites thought about federalism—shifting its focus from protecting civil liberties to guaranteeing property rights. A principal lesson for the Reconstruction generation was that national action was important to protect racial and cultural minorities from state action. The Founding Fathers, however, had another model in mind. They saw the national government as the greater danger to personal freedom and the states as more troublesome when it came to property interests. Thus, they applied the Bill of Rights only to the federal government and inserted clauses into the rest of the text that expressly limited how the states could regulate property.[48] The backlash against the Pullman Strike reinforced the older understanding of federalism by presenting a clear example, at least in conservative eyes, of a state governor acting as an enemy of property. This view was not born in 1894—it was well represented on the Supreme Court by the dissenters in *Slaughter-House* and by scholars who argued that the proper reading of the Fourteenth Amendment was that it did secure property and contract rights from state action. My point is that this view was bolstered by the events in Chicago, the influence of which soon became apparent on the Court.

At the same time, the unrest was a poor advertisement for the idea of extending the substantive parts of the Bill of Rights (with the exception of the Takings Clause) to state action. As early as 1886, the Court expressed concern in an incorporation case about the need to protect "the right of the state to disperse assemblages organized for sedition and treason, and the right to suppress armed mobs bent on riot and rapine."[49] The prospect of broadened free speech rights, expanded gun ownership, or more freedom from searches and seizures was not especially attractive when state law enforcement looked like the only thing standing between order and chaos. Common wisdom holds that civil liberties contract in wartime, but few pause to consider that serious internal disturbances can have the same effect. The Pullman Strike did just that for incorporation and gave its critics ammunition for the next round of litigation.

Populism and the Invention of Jim Crow

While President Cleveland was deploying troops to hold back the swelling tide of discontent, southern Democrats called for white solidarity to trump the Populist theme of interracial cooperation based on class.[50] The surge in racial hatred for political

purposes coincided with the passage of the first wave of segregation laws regulating the seating of railroad passengers. Though
the backlash against agrarian reform was not the only factor in
the birth of Jim Crow, it was a significant factor.

Scholars agree that the system of legal segregation in the
South began with the railroad statutes passed in the 1890s, but
not on why they were enacted at that time. In part, this disagreement is due to the lack of available legislative materials. Some
argue that the push for stronger federal protection of African
American voting rights in the unsuccessful "Force Bill" of 1890
angered white southerners and was the catalyst for Jim Crow.[51]
Others contend that the children of the freed slaves were far
more assertive when it came to their rights than their parents
had been, and that this generational shift led to an overwhelming racist response.[52] A third possibility is that these statutes
were a reaction to the Populists.[53]

Without discounting the importance of the first two factors,
I want to explain why the link to Populism rings true. First, the
choice of railroads as the target of the initial segregation laws is
suggestive. Rural activists were particularly interested in regulating railroads, and with Jim Crow laws, conservatives could
throw them a bone while driving a wedge between supporters
of interracial politics.[54] Second, the evolution of these statutes
throughout the South points to a Populist connection. The following states enacted the first batch of mandatory segregation

laws for all railroad cars: Mississippi (1888), Louisiana (1890), Texas (1891), Alabama (1891), Arkansas (1891), Tennessee (1891), Georgia (1891), and Kentucky (1892).[55] This lawmaking occurred while the Farmers' Alliance and the Populist Party were gaining ground but not yet in control, and many of these states (especially Texas, Alabama, and Georgia) were hotbeds of Populism. But between 1892 and 1898, no Jim Crow railroad statutes were passed, and this period coincided with Populist control (usually in partnership with the Republicans) of legislatures such as North Carolina's and Maryland's.[56] After that, segregation returned with a vengeance and spread through the remaining states as Populism was snuffed out.[57] Accordingly, there was at least some connection between the virulence of racial segregation and the political clout of the Populists.

Inferring causation between the appearance of Jim Crow and conservative resistance to the Populist movement is also justified because aggressive white supremacy was at the heart of both. As the author of a study of Florida politics during this period observed: "The Populists came to be known in the conservative press as 'nigger-worshippers,' and the 'nigger party.'"[58] Voters in Alabama were told that if the Democrats lost, African American "children shall sit side by side with children with white faces and straight hair, and social equality will be the inevitable result."[59] In North Carolina, the claim was that a Populist victory meant "negroes in every office, mixed schools, intermarriage, [and] social equality."[60] In short, in Tom Watson's words, "the argument against the independent political movement in the South may be boiled down to one word—nigger."[61]

When soliciting votes through racial appeals did not work, the Democratic establishment turned to fraud and that other tried-and-true solution—violence. Lynching surged during the early 1890s, and Populists faced physical intimidation at rallies and at the polls.[62] Indeed, for one scholar, "the sudden and dramatic rise in the lynching of black men in and after 1889 stands out like some giant volcanic eruption on the landscape of Southern race relations."[63] Vote fraud sometimes paid dividends—Watson's congressional seat was essentially stolen from him in 1892—but the strategy was difficult to hide and provoked criticism that was damaging.[64] Eventually, anti-Populist forces concluded that they should end African American and poor white voting entirely, but that radical step did not succeed across the South until after Bryan's defeat in 1896.

A vivid example of the fear in southern Democratic ranks can be found in a private letter from the governor of Georgia imploring President Cleveland to soften his hard line on the gold standard. According to the governor, "the conditions of this State are fearful and threatening," and "the long-continued delay in helpful legislation by Congress" was helping the Populists.[65] Thus, Democrats were "rapidly losing strength in this State. Every election held in the State for the past three (3) months has gone against the Democratic party and in favor of the Populists."[66]

The letter concluded with a warning that "ex-Congressman Watson, the leader of the Populists, has taken advantage of the conditions, and is speaking over the State to assemblies never less than 2,000, and sometimes as many as 5,000 people." The voters were about to intervene.

Stalemate at the Polls

As Watson had predicted, the president's escalation of his resistance to the Populists strained the two-party system on the eve of the 1894 midterm election. A military officer involved in the Pullman crackdown reflected the intense divisions of the age by explaining that "men must take sides . . . either for anarchy, secret enclaves, unwritten law, mob violence, and universal chaos under the red or white flag of socialism on the one hand; or on the side of established government."[67] The Populists taunted Cleveland for "bunco[ing] the country in a huge confidence game" and embraced the radical mantra that "to make an omelet, you must break some eggs."[68] And by 1894 the "Populists had reason to forecast that the Democratic party, caught in the middle as the country polarized, would be pulled apart—just as the Whigs had been split by another polarization forty years before—and the country would be left with two parties, Populists and Republicans."[69]

Both sides could point to electoral evidence that they would prevail. Populists were pleased because they increased their overall vote share over 1892.[70] The main beneficiary of Democratic disarray, however, was the Republican Party, which has been absent from the story so far but now seized its chance to grab control of the House of Representatives.[71] Cleveland's resistance had not doused the flames of Populism. Instead, he split the country and provoked the leaders of each side to increase their demands. One conservative suggested a way out of the deadlock: "What shall minister to a mind diseased like the Populist's? Only constitutional remedies."[72] The Supreme Court was about to put its fist on the scale.

FOUR

The Supreme Court Intervenes

> The present assault upon capital is but the beginning. It will be
> but the stepping-stone to others, larger and more sweeping, till
> our political contests will become a war of the poor against the
> rich; a war constantly growing in intensity and bitterness.
> —Justice Stephen J. Field

Conventional wisdom holds that the Supreme Court is the most important institution in constitutional law, but at generational turning points the Court is just another source of conservative resistance. Justice Robert H. Jackson, who was a close advisor to President Franklin D. Roosevelt during his battle with the Justices, said afterward that courts are "the check of a preceding generation on the present one; a check of conservative legal philosophy upon a dynamic people, and nearly always the check of a rejected regime on the one in being. This conservative institution is under every pressure and temptation to throw its weight against novel programs and untried policies which win popular elections."[1] From 1894 to 1896 the Justices succumbed to this temptation and issued a series of unprecedented decisions that were linked by their support for opponents of the Populists. The

Court's decision to play the constitutional trump card was the latest escalation of this generational struggle and set the stage for the 1896 campaign.[2]

Preemptive Opinions and Judicial Resistance

Most of the time, courts and politicians approach constitutional issues differently, but as the fight between generations reaches its peak that distinction virtually disappears. A typical description of the judicial process goes something like this. Courts pay no attention to the legal arguments or to the political fortunes of grass-roots activists. Judges carefully follow precedent and avoid deciding anything that is unnecessary to resolve a case. And they certainly do not comment about the platforms of parties or presidents. After all, judges are professionals applying the rule of law—this is a fundamental principle of American democracy.

At moments of great constitutional stress, however, these standards of restraint are discarded in favor of a more aggressive approach.[3] For all of their legal training, the Justices are ultimately political appointees who owe their selection to a particular party and represent its legal ideology, though there are some exceptions. When a massive popular mobilization occurs in support of ideas that are sharply at odds with the prior consensus, the Court almost never stands back and just lets the process play out within the bounds of precedent. Instead, the Justices jump into the fray just as elected officials of the same generation do: by seeking opportunities to declare the goals of the new movement invalid and to hurt its chances at the polls. While this partisan behavior should be criticized, it is unrealistic to pretend that it never happens.[4]

Indeed, at nearly every transition point between constitutional generations there is what I call a "preemptive opinion," which is a decision in which the Court engages in an act of massive resistance and crafts new doctrine that is specifically targeted at the rising popular movement. These rare preemptive-opinion cases, such as *Worcester v. Georgia* (in which John Marshall distorted the law to save the Cherokees and criticize President Jackson) and *Dred Scott v. Sandford* (in which Chief Justice Roger Taney distorted the law to find part of the Republican Party's platform unconstitutional), display three unusual traits.[5] First, the Justices decide almost every issue in the litigation as broadly as possible. The normal presumption of judicial modesty is set aside because the Court is eager to make a political statement. Second, the Court ignores precedent if applying it means giving the new generation a political win. A similar dynamic drove President Cleveland to overlook states' rights and adopt a new Commerce Clause theory in response to the Pullman Strike. Finally, because the Court must go well beyond precedent to take a blatantly ideological stand, it needs to invent a new doctrine to support the result. Most of the time, a preemptive opinion does not stand for long because the rising generation overwhelms judicial resistance by winning elections and putting its supporters on the Court. In the 1890s, though, these sweeping cases established the constitutional architecture for decades to come because Bryan lost.

The Overture: *Reagan* and *E. C. Knight*

The first sign that the political winds swirling around the Court were having an impact came in *Reagan v. Farmers' Loan and Trust Co.*, which was an 1894 case challenging railroad rates set by Texas.[6] In contrast to decisions over the previous twenty years, in *Reagan* the Justices held that the rates at issue were void under the Fourteenth Amendment because the railroad could not make enough money to pay its debt or a fair return to its shareholders.[7] After stating that "there is nothing new or strange in this," which is what judges often say before they do something new or strange, the Court explained that the Equal Protection Clause barred state laws "by which the property of one individual is, without compensation, wrested from him for the benefit of another, or of the public."[8] Moreover, in *Reagan* the Court took the position that the state's justifications for its low rate ceilings—for example, that farmers desperately needed relief because of the panic—were not adequate and distorted market principles.[9] This decision received little attention, for the ruling allowed the state to adopt a new rate schedule. Nevertheless, *Reagan* marked an important change in judicial attitudes toward state regulation and wealth redistribution that would soon bear fruit.

Another shot across the Populist bow came a year later in *United States v. E. C. Knight*, which raised the question of whether the sugar trust was subject to the Sherman Antitrust Act.[10] The trust controlled 98 percent of the market, and Senator Sherman himself declared it one of the two most dangerous monopolies (the other was Pullman) because sugar was a necessity of life.[11] The issue before the Court was whether the trust fell within the statutory language regulating combinations that restrained "commerce among the several states." The Court's decision in *E. C. Knight* held that the Sherman Act did not cover the trust, because sugar production was manufacturing instead of commerce. Chief Justice Fuller, writing for the Court, said that "commerce succeeds to manufacture, and is not a part of it."[12] Although "the power to control the manufacture of a given thing involves in a certain sense the control of its disposition . . . [and] may result in bringing the operation of commerce into play, it does not control it, and affects it only incidentally and indirectly."[13] He also expressed concern that the line between federal and state authority would be obliterated if a broad definition of commerce were adopted; he said it was "vital that the independence of the commercial power and of the police power, and the delimitation between them, however sometimes perplexing, should always be recognized."[14]

This narrow interpretation of commerce attracted broad support within the Court, but two aspects of *E. C. Knight* are worth pondering. First, the opinion paid virtually no attention to Chief Justice Marshall's "landmark" decision in *Gibbons;* it mentioned the case just twice in passing.[15] This neglect reinforces the observation made in chapter 2 that *Gibbons* was not significant in its time and that it was the Populists, not the legendary Chief Justice, who turned the Commerce Clause into the key for unlocking congressional authority. Second, the Court in *E. C. Knight* went out of its way to attack nationalization in a very unjudicial manner, quoting a Dormant Commerce Clause case from a decade earlier, which stated that if commerce included manufactures, then "Congress would be invested . . . with the power to regulate, not only manufactures, but also agriculture, horticulture, stock raising, domestic fisheries, mining—in short, every branch of human industry."[16] In the Court's view, "Any movement toward the establishment of rules of production in this vast country, with its many different climates and opportunities, could only be at the sacrifice of the peculiar advantages of a large part of the localities in it."[17] Indeed, that centralized outcome "would be about the widest possible departure from the declared object" of the Commerce Clause.[18]

E. C. Knight reads like a direct response to the Populist agenda and to the party's view of the Commerce Clause. The Court made a textbook argument against nationalization and drew no distinction between the meaning of commerce in the Sherman

Act and in the Constitution, which implied that there was a constitutional obstacle to public ownership at the federal level. Yet judicial resistance was still cautious at this stage, perhaps because trust regulation was more popular than the heart of the Populist agenda. After all, the Justices did not discuss railroads, the telegraph, or the telephone, which were the instrumentalities that the Populists wanted to nationalize. Thus, this case also generated little comment in the press or in the political world.

Nonetheless, the trajectory of the majority's thinking was not lost on Justice Harlan. In his lone dissent he cited *Gibbons* for the point that Congress had broad authority to act whenever commerce was affected. Today this conclusion seems obvious, but at the time it represented a significant innovation.[19] Refuting *E. C. Knight*'s line between manufacturing and commerce, he wrote that "it is equally true that when manufacture ends, that which has been manufactured becomes a subject of commerce; that buying and selling succeed manufacture, come into existence after the process of manufacture is completed, precede transportation, and are as much commercial intercourse" as moving purchased goods.[20] Harlan added that he was "unable to perceive that [the act] would imperil the autonomy of the States, especially as that result cannot be attained through the action of any one State."[21] Antitrust regulation was almost impossible for a state because a firm could just relocate and because any state's attempt to regulate a trust's operations beyond that state's borders might run afoul of the Dormant Commerce Clause.

As Justice Harlan was setting forth sound arguments against the Court's doctrinal view, he also joined the broader constitutional debate by embracing the Populist vision of the Commerce Clause. In words that tracked the logic of James B. Weaver, the party's presidential candidate in 1892, Harlan said that *E. C. Knight* undermined one "primary object of the Union, which was to place commerce among the States under the control of the common government of all the people, and thereby relieve or protect it against burdens or restrictions imposed, by whatever authority, for the benefit of particular localities or special interests."[22] He responded to the majority's concern about nationalizing industry by embracing the popular call for action against the danger posed by large corporations. Indeed, he said these "overshadowing combinations" were "governed entirely by the law of greed and selfishness—so powerful that no single State is able to overthrow them . . . and so all-pervading that they threaten the integrity of our institutions."[23] Harlan's strong comments drew little attention, but within a few months critics were condemning him for espousing radicalism from the bench when he said similar things about the Court's attack on the federal income tax.

Pollock and the Income Tax

The Court's opening jabs at the Populists were modest (as the lack of a reaction against them shows), but the dynamic of mutual transformation was at work. When the income tax sponsored by William Jennings Bryan and enacted in 1894 was attacked as unconstitutional in *Pollock v. Farmers' Loan and Trust Co.*, the Justices were told that drastic action was essential to prevent a Populist takeover.[24] The resulting preemptive opinions showed just how far the Court was willing to bend the rules out of fear of what the new generation would do.

Almost nobody prior to *Pollock* thought that Congress lacked the authority to impose an income tax.[25] Only thirteen years earlier, in *Springer v. United States*, the Justices had unanimously upheld an income tax enacted during the Civil War.[26] Moreover, the Court had never invalidated a federal tax on constitutional grounds despite many invitations to do so.[27] All of these unsuccessful challenges said the same thing—that the tax at issue did not meet the requirements of the Direct Tax Clauses, which state that head taxes and other "direct Taxes shall be apportioned among the several states . . . according to their respective Numbers."[28] Thus, a direct tax cannot be collected unless it is divided among the states according to each state's share of the population. This mandate would make an income tax politically unpalatable by requiring that tax rates vary from state to state (with higher taxes in the poorer states) to generate the proper amount of revenue.

One reason that the Court was reluctant to describe taxes as "direct" was that the original purpose of the provision was to block the taxation of slaves. In the first case construing the

Direct Tax Clauses, *Hylton v. United States*, Justice William Paterson, who had been a member of the Constitutional Convention, explained that because the South had many slaves and the North had few, "the southern states, if no provision had been introduced in the constitution, would have been wholly at the mercy of the other states. Congress in such case, might tax slaves."[29] By inserting the Direct Tax Clauses into the text and providing that head taxes (and thus slave taxes) were direct, the Framers forced the North to share in those taxes rather than placing the burden exclusively on the South. The Thirteenth Amendment, of course, rendered these clauses meaningless with respect to their original purpose.[30]

When a corporate shareholder objected to the income tax and sought equitable relief, however, the great conservative lawyers of the day urged the Justices to give the Direct Tax Clauses a new anti-redistribution reading. Joseph H. Choate, a leader of the corporate bar, took up the case because he believed that unless he built "a rampart around the rights of property," the Populist Party would establish a dangerous new order.[31] He told the Court that upholding the tax would be "the beginning of socialism and communism" and would cause "the destruction of the Constitution itself."[32] Opposing counsel responded that the income tax should be upheld because the "people have become arrayed in hostile political ranks upon a question which all men feel is not a question of law, but of legislation."[33] Choate was emotional in his rebuttal: "If it be true, as my friend said

Joseph H. Choate, the
lawyer who argued
*Pollock v. Farmers' Loan
and Trust Co.* and revived
Marbury v. Madison.
Library of Congress.

in closing, that the passions of the people are aroused on this subject, if it be true that a mighty army of sixty million citizens is likely to be incensed by this decision, it is more vital to the future welfare of this country that this court again resolutely and courageously declare, as Marshall did, that it *has* the power to set aside an act of Congress violative of the Constitution, and that it will not hesitate in executing that power, no matter what the threatened consequences of popular or populistic wrath may be."[34]

As Justice Harlan said in his dissent, Choate all but urged the Court "to stand in the breach for the protection of the just rights of property against the advancing hosts of socialism."[35]

The Justices were approaching the same point of no return that Cleveland had faced two years earlier. Should they join with reformers and help moderate their demands or fight back and risk institutional damage from an enraged opposition?

The Court chose the path of most resistance. In declaring the 1894 income tax unconstitutional, it deviated from professional norms to such an extent that Charles Evans Hughes, the Chief Justice during the New Deal, called *Pollock* a self-inflicted wound of the same magnitude as *Dred Scott*.[36] To begin with, the Court's holding was problematic because it had no authority to grant injunctive relief in tax cases. As four dissenters noted, a federal statute barred courts from enjoining the collection of federal taxes.[37] Indeed, the law was clear that a disgruntled taxpayer was required to pay the disputed tax and then sue for damages. Accordingly, the correct disposition of the case was a dismissal without reaching the merits. The Court's answer was that the "question of jurisdiction, for the purposes of the case, was explicitly waived on the argument."[38] Even assuming that a jurisdictional defect could be waived, which was unlikely given the limited authority of Article III courts, judges normally do not decide controversial issues unless they must. Then again, if the Justices had dismissed *Pollock* in this way, there would have been no major ruling lambasting the Populists before the 1896 election.

Another unusual feature of *Pollock* supports the hypothesis that the Justices were chafing to attack the Populists and ignored the usual restraints. When the case was first argued, one member of the Court was ill and not present. As a result, the initial opinion in *Pollock* addressed only taxes on income from real estate and municipal bonds.[39] After the ill Justice returned, the Court granted a petition for rehearing—a rare event—and expanded its prior holding by declaring that all income taxes were direct.[40] Once again, this activism was inconsistent with the norms of judicial process, but granting the rehearing petition did enhance *Pollock*'s political impact. The force of the Populist assault was driving a majority of the Justices into more and more extraordinary resistance.

After clearing through these procedural impediments, the Court began its substantive analysis by quoting *Marbury* for the proposition that constitutional review is "the very essence of judicial duty."[41] To a modern ear, this sounds unremarkable. In fact, it was yet another revolutionary move—much like the embrace of the Commerce Clause—that is obscured by the lack of attention given to the Populist failure. Davison M. Douglas points out that the Justices never cited *Marbury* to support an exercise of judicial review until the 1890s, and that most commentators referred to the case as authority only for original jurisdiction, writs of mandamus, and other technical matters.[42] This limited reading seems impossible given the reverence that Marshall's opinion receives now, but consider that *Dred Scott*, which was the first case after *Marbury* to strike down an act of Congress, did not refer to *Marbury* at all. Maybe the omission should not be surprising, though, given the similar obscurity of *Gibbons*, which was another of Marshall's supposed landmark opinions.

During the 1890s, *Marbury* enjoyed a revival, which Douglas attributes to the firestorm surrounding *Pollock* and the need to find some way to defend the opinion from Populist attacks.[43] With this background, the peroration of Choate's oral argument, in which he alluded to *Marbury* and Marshall's defense of judicial review against the political attacks of Jefferson, is revealed as strategically brilliant, not rhetorically hollow. The Court reached for the lifeline that Choate provided, and *Pollock* represents the first time *Marbury* was used to justify the invalidation of a federal statute.[44] In one sense, this was a defensive gesture. Since (as will soon be clear) *Pollock* rested on weak grounds, the Court needed every bit of authority that it could get its hands on to support the holding. Ironically, the search for that support was the start of canonization for the most famous case in American law.

Marbury's transformation during the 1890s is part of a broader phenomenon whereby the friction between constitutional generations produces innovations that begin as political tools but can develop into foundational principles. In other words, constitutional law is far less deliberate than we might think. The heat of battle and the desire for victory compel each side in the generational cycle to throw out new arguments and theories to achieve its goals, and most of the time nobody pauses to consider the long-term implications of the proposed actions.[45] Only time and selective memory raise certain acts to the level of wisdom—a process captured by the line (generally attributed to Harry Truman) that "a statesman is a dead politician."[46] The reinvention of the Commerce Clause is one example from this period, and the revival of *Marbury* is another.

After introducing *Marbury* as the lodestone for judicial review, the Court bared its teeth and set aside long-standing doctrine to void a federal tax for the first time. Mustering a set of lackluster quotations from the Framers, eighteenth-century economists, and English cases on direct taxes, the Court held that the Direct Tax Clauses were actually meant "to prevent an attack upon accumulated property by mere force of numbers."[47] Indeed, their provisions were "one of the bulwarks of private rights and private property."[48] This claim was unimpressive because the Court ignored the real purpose of these clauses, which was to protect slavery, while conceding that there was no real authority to support the contention that income taxes were direct.[49] Besides, Justice Harlan in his dissent observed that the materials cited by the Court were "several times directly brought to the attention of this court" and had been rejected every time.[50]

The majority's lack of professionalism only grew worse when the Justices tried to run the gauntlet established by the Court's precedents, which stated that only head and land taxes were direct.[51] In fact, the challenge for those seeking to attack the income tax law was even tougher because in some cases the Court had expressly stated that income taxes were not direct.[52] In *Pollock* the Court distinguished these decisions by calling the statements dicta. The Court had a harder time dealing with *Hylton*—the first decision that construed the Direct Tax Clauses as applying to only land and head taxes—and resorted to the preposterous claim that "the case is badly reported" and therefore should not be read as authority against extending those provisions to income taxes.[53] As for *Springer*, the case in which the Court upheld the Civil War income tax, it "grew out of the war of the rebellion . . . and [was] abandoned as soon after the war was ended as it could be done safely."[54] By contrast, again according to *Pollock*, the present tax was enacted "in a time of profound peace," which "furnishes an additional reason for circumspection and care in disposing of the case."[55] Yet nothing in *Springer* indicated that the Court's decision rested on an emergency or wartime rationale, and in any event it is hard to see the relevance of this distinction for the Direct Tax Clauses.[56]

The dissenters in *Pollock* and academic commentators criticized this flagrant disregard for precedent as an assault on the rule of law. In Justice Edward White's assessment, "the result of the opinion . . . just announced is to overthrow a long and consistent line of decisions, and to deny to the legislative department of the government the possession of a power conceded to it by universal consensus for one hundred years."[57] The *Harvard Law Review* thoroughly agreed: it said that the Justices had rendered "an opinion in which is laid down a doctrine that is contrary to what has been accepted as law for nearly one hundred years."[58] Justice

Harlan made a similar point in more understated language: "It seems to me that the court has not given to the maxim of *stare decisis* the full effect to which it is entitled."[59] Another dissenting Justice claimed that the decision was "the most disastrous blow ever struck at the constitutional power of Congress."[60]

According to many observers, *Pollock*'s radical break with precedent was justified to defeat the Populist Party, as the Court "began to regard itself as the last defense of the country against socialism."[61] Justice Field's concurring opinion was the most explicit about this motive, as we see in the epigraph to this chapter: he explained that the "war of the poor against the rich" was "constantly growing in intensity and bitterness." With this statement, Field was acknowledging that the process of mutual transformation was under way and that he was not immune to the pressures of escalation. His unique contribution was to declare an income tax an "arbitrary discrimination" and argue for the equivalence of racial, religious, and wealth discrimination. As he put it, "Whenever a distinction is made in the burdens a law imposes or in the benefits it confers on any citizens by reason of their birth, or wealth, or religion, it is class legislation, and leads inevitably to oppression and abuses, and to general unrest and disturbance in society."[62] This declaration was consistent with his view in *Slaughter-House* that the Fourteenth Amendment should protect property rights from state action, and in *Pollock* he tried to expand that concept to federal action (although the textual basis for expansion was not clear).

The *Pollock* dissenters saw what was going on and faulted the Court for getting caught up in politics, though that left them open to the charge that they were doing the same thing on behalf of the Populists. Justice Henry Brown used his opinion to decry the influence of the "spectre of socialism" on the decision, but the real fireworks came from Justice Harlan, who pounded the bench with his fist as he delivered his dissent.[63] The best way of conveying the impact of his rhetoric is with a sampling of the critical commentary in the press. The *New York Times* said: "Lawyers who have practiced for years before the Supreme Court say they never before listened to such revolutionary statements from the bench. The most rampant Populist could not have . . . shown greater contempt for the views of the majority than Justice Harlan did in [his] long harangue."[64] The *Chicago Tribune* said: "Justice Harlan led off with a sensational address which will make him the Presidential candidate of the Populist party next year if he cares for the empty honor."[65] And *The Nation* said: "The heat with which Justice Harlan expounded the Marx gospel from the bench showed that the brake [on Populism] was applied none too soon. The Judge's observations on the need of the tax to keep the rich in their places was as odd as anything that has fallen from a court."[66]

One thing was clear after *Pollock:* the Court was now an active player in a national constitutional dialogue. The income tax case became "a topic of heated discussion in every bank, barbershop, and barroom" and would be a key issue in Bryan's presidential campaign.[67]

Debs and the Shadow of Revolution

Not long after the rulings in *E. C. Knight* and *Pollock*, the leaders of the Pullman Strike brought their fight with President Cleveland to the Supreme Court. For refusing to obey the injunction against the strike, Eugene V. Debs and his associates were found guilty of criminal contempt. The prisoners sought a writ of habeas corpus and put together a star-studded legal team led by former senator Lyman Trumbull and Clarence Darrow, who would eventually clash with Bryan in the Scopes trial.[68] Like the lawyers in *Pollock*, the advocates for Debs used pointed language to warn the Justices that upholding the injunction would only inflame popular opinion. Trumbull told the Court that "refusing to work for a railroad is no crime . . . And though such action may incidentally delay the mails or interfere with interstate commerce, it being a lawful act and not done for the purpose, it is no offense."[69] His co-counsel added that any attempt to crush the constitutional insurgents would fuel "dynamic social forces until they gather an accumulated and resistless energy by such compression [and] precipitate an explosion which shall wreck the social order."[70]

What made the Court's decision in *Debs* remarkable was not its result, which was unanimous, but the breadth of the opinion that was issued against the strike leaders. The lower court upheld the injunction under the Sherman Act because the strikers were acting to obstruct interstate commerce.[71] Instead of adopting this modest view, the Justices rested their conclusion on constitutional grounds. The Court framed the issue as whether the "relations of the general government to interstate commerce and the transportation of the mails as such authorized a direct interference to prevent a forcible obstruction thereof."[72] In other words, the Justices responded to the Pullman Strike by writing limits on strikes into the Constitution.

The Court's holding was based on the idea that the Dormant Commerce Clause gave the president the power to remove private as well as state-sponsored barriers to interstate commerce. In *Debs* the Court reasoned that if "a state with its recognized powers of sovereignty is impotent to obstruct interstate commerce, can it be that any mere voluntary association of individuals within the limits of that State has a power that the State itself does not possess?"[73] Not only was the Court's answer a resounding no, but the Justices offered a fervent defense of President Cleveland, stating that "the strong arm of the national government may be put forth to brush away all obstructions . . . If the emergency arises, the army of the Nation, and all its militia, are at the service of the nation, to compel obedience to its laws."[74] Thus, the Court had held, in the space of just a few months, that Congress lacked the power under the Commerce Clause to regulate the sugar trust (*E. C. Knight*) but that the president possessed inherent (and unilateral) commerce authority to break strikes (*Debs*).

The inconsistency between *E. C. Knight* and *Debs* was striking, but the connection between them was simple: hostility to Populism. Indeed, the political tenor of *Debs* was evident in the Court's discussion of why an injunction backed by contempt sanctions was a valid remedy. The strike leaders argued that they were being deprived of their Sixth Amendment right to a jury trial by the use of contempt proceedings that let courts impose a sentence without a jury. Their brief said, "No more tyrannous and arbitrary government can be devised than the administration of criminal law by a single judge by means of injunction and proceedings in contempt."[75] Furthermore, the case law provided that an injunction could not be issued unless the ordinary processes of law were unavailable. In this instance, however, state and federal tribunals were available, even if it was hard to bring a successful criminal case, because—and this was a key point of Trumbull and Darrow's argument—it was not clear that the strike leaders had violated any law.

The Court's answer in *Debs* was an amazing rebuke to popular government. It said that the ordinary processes of law were not open because sympathetic local juries could not be relied upon to punish strikers who blocked commerce. In other words, "If all the inhabitants of a state, or even a great body of them, should combine to obstruct interstate commerce or the transportation of the mails, prosecutions for such offenses . . . in such a community would be doomed in advance to failure."[76] Unless federal officials had other means of enforcing their will, "the whole interests of the nation in these respects would be at the absolute mercy of a portion of the inhabitants of that single state."[77] This novel presumption of jury nullification was another example of how the Pullman Strike pushed elites to rewrite the law out of fear of local threats to property rights. Juries were now dangerous.

As the opinion reached its climax, the Court used blunt rhetoric to tell the country that radicalism should be rejected: "If ever there was a special exigency, one which demanded that the court should do all that courts can do, it was disclosed by this bill, and we need not turn to the public history of the day, which only reaffirms with clearest emphasis all its allegations."[78] The Court went on to demonize the strikers: "It is a lesson which cannot be learned too soon or too thoroughly that under this government . . . no wrong, real or fancied, carries with it legal warrant to invite as a means of redress the cooperation of a mob, with its accompanying acts of violence."[79] This conservative vision was applauded by the *Chicago Tribune*, which said *Debs* served as "a notice to all Anarchists and other disturbers of the public peace that the hands of the General Government are not fettered."[80]

Though *Debs* receives plenty of attention for its discussion of the Commerce Clause, its implications for the incorporation of the Bill of Rights are overlooked. If an express constitutional right like jury trial could not stand against the claim that civil order was in peril, then how could the extension of that right (or almost any part of the Bill of Rights) to the states proceed? More important, the Court's validation of federal injunctions against strikes inflicted serious damage on First Amendment principles by barring workers from persuading their fellow citizens through direct action.[81] In sum, *Debs* crystallized the doubts created by the Pullman Strike about the wisdom of giving more protection—procedural and substantive—against state action at a time when local law enforcement concerns were intense.

The author of *Debs* was Justice David Brewer, and his shifting views in the 1890s are indicative of the evolution in the legal culture caused by the campaign against the Populists and against labor organizers. In 1892, Brewer was one of the dissenters in *O'Neil* who concluded that the Fourteenth Amendment applied the Cruel and Unusual Punishments Clause of the Eighth Amendment to the states. At the same time, he was a critic of Populism. Dissenting from another 1892 case that upheld state regulation of grain elevator rates, Brewer stated: "The paternal theory of government is to me odious. If it may regulate the price of one service which is not a public service, or the compensation for the use of one kind of property, which is not devoted to a public use, why may it not with equal reason regulate the price of all service, and the compensation to be paid for the use of all property? And, if so, 'Looking Backward' is nearer than a dream."[82] His direct reference to the novel that endorsed nationalization and was a bible for the protest movement shows

Justice David Brewer, author of
In re Debs. Library of Congress.
Photo by Frances Benjamin
Johnston.

that Brewer was paying close attention to what was going on in the nation. The problem was that Brewer's support for incorporation was in tension with his concern about preserving property rights.

When push came to shove, Brewer chose order over freedom. His approach in *Debs* was foreshadowed by a speech he gave two years earlier in which he said: "Who does not hear the old demagogic cry, '*Vox Populi vox Dei*' . . . constantly invoked to justify disregard of those guaranties which have hitherto been deemed sufficient to give protection to private property?"[83] Denouncing the "black flag of anarchism" and the "red flag of socialism," he concluded by asking: "Who does not see the wide unrest that fills the land; who does not feel that vast social changes are impending, and realize that those changes must be guided in justice to safety and peace or they will culminate in revolution?"[84] His conversion would be complete by 1900, when he reversed his position in *O'Neil* and joined the Court's decision in *Maxwell*, rejecting incorporation and rewriting *Slaughter-House*.

As with *Pollock*, the Court's decision in *Debs* was unpopular with reformers and hailed by conservatives. Governor Altgeld, who had opposed the president's intervention during the Pullman Strike, said the Justices were turning the republic into a government by decree, and "the corrupt money power has its withering finger on every pulse in the land."[85] The money power, he went on, "sits in the White House and legislates in the capitol. Courts of justice are its ministers and legislatures are its lackeys."[86] Eugene V. Debs asked why the Court had stabbed the "Magna Charta of American liberty to death in the interest of corporations, that labor might be disrobed of its inalienable rights and those who advocated its claim to justice imprisoned as if they were felons."[87] Taking the opposite point of view, *The Nation* sardonically praised the strikers: "Debs, Altgeld & Co. have thus unconsciously rendered the country a great service by their course last year, for it is an immense gain to have so important a principle of constitutional construction definitely settled."[88] The comment expresses, once again, the logic of escalation during generational conflicts and summarizes how the Supreme Court handled the Pullman Strike: Whatever you can do, I can do better.[89]

Plessy and the Populist Resistance

The last case that must be assessed in the context of judicial resistance to Populism is *Plessy*. My decision to group the case enshrining the "separate but equal" doctrine with *E. C. Knight, Debs,* and *Pollock* is unorthodox. The typical view of *Plessy* holds that the opinion was unaffected by national politics (although it came down in the crucial year of 1896) and had nothing to do with Populism.[90] And it is true that there were no procedural irregularities or overt references to politics in *Plessy* as there were in *Pollock* or *Debs*. Nonetheless, there are some notable links between these cases.

In essence, *Plessy* validated the resistance to the Populists in the South. Conservative opposition to agrarian reform was almost certainly one of the factors supporting the rise of Jim Crow in the 1890s. By upholding Louisiana's version of railroad segregation against a Fourteenth Amendment attack, the Justices threw their weight behind the strategy of using race to drive a wedge into the reform coalition. This point is implied in Justice Harlan's dissent in *Plessy,* in which he criticized the state statute: "What can more certainly arouse race hate, what can certainly create and perpetuate a feeling of distrust between these races, than state enactments which, in fact, proceed on the ground that colored citizens are so inferior and degraded that they cannot be allowed to sit in public coaches occupied by white citizens?"[91] In other words, segregation laws either were intended to breed mistrust between the races or were very likely to. What is left unclear is why anyone would want to create mistrust. The answer, in part, is that southern Democrats were trying to stop the Populists.[92] I cannot prove that the Court was aware of this motivation when it handed down the *Plessy* decision, nor can I say that the decision was a distortion of the doctrine, intended to achieve a political result. What I can say is that *Plessy* aided the enemies of Populism just as much as, if not more than, *Pollock* did.

A connection between the ongoing political turmoil and the *Plessy* decision is also suggested by the press coverage of the case. In an editorial entitled "Equality, but Not Socialism," the *New Orleans Daily Picayune* said: "Equality of rights does not mean community of rights . . . If all rights were common as well as equal, there would be practically no such thing as private property, private life, or social distinctions, but all would belong to everybody who might choose to use it. This would be absolute socialism, in which the individual would be extinguished in the vast mass of human-being, a condition repugnant to every principle of enlightened democracy."[93] This argument in favor of Jim Crow sounds a lot like an attack on Populist economics. Maybe this was just a coincidence, but that seems unlikely given that conservatives saw the Populists in the South as advocates for so-cial equality across the board.

Putting *Plessy* alongside the major cases generated by the Populist revolt is helpful because it recasts how stare decisis was discussed in *Brown v. Board of Education*.[94] Chief Justice Warren rested the Court's judgment striking down segregation in public schools on the increasing importance of education, which is often criticized as a weak (or unduly pragmatic) rationale. Whether the argument needs buttressing or not, viewing *Plessy* as part of a set of related decisions made in response to the same political upheaval offers new support for *Brown*. By 1954, none of the anti-Populist opinions (*E. C. Knight*, *Debs*, or *Pollock*) were good law except for *Plessy*. At this higher level of generality, where we look at precedent from a temporal or generational perspective, we can see that the erosion in *Plessy*'s foundation was severe by the 1950s.

Finally, setting *Plessy* within its broader constitutional context allows us to see just how fragile the ruling was. In this sense, *Brown* and *Plessy* are alike. Both rested on plausible interpretations of the pertinent authorities but could not become settled law without the support of local and federal elected officials. The fact that *Brown* was unanimous (and *Plessy* nearly so) certainly influenced the debate that followed, but did not determine its outcome. Modern lawyers grasp this point with regard to *Brown*, but they fail to make the connection with *Plessy*. Yet this idea was not lost on Thurgood Marshall and the other NAACP lawyers who argued *Brown*. Listen to their analysis: "*Plessy v. Ferguson* chilled the development in the South of opinion conducive to the acceptance of Negroes on the basis of equality because those of the white South desiring to afford Negroes the egalitarian status which the Civil War Amendments had hoped to achieve were barred by state law from acting in accordance with their beliefs. In this connection, it is significant that the Populist movement flourished for a short period during the 1890's and threatened to take over political control of the South through a coalition of the poor Negro and poor white farmers. This movement was completely smashed and since *Plessy v. Ferguson* no similar phenomenon has taken hold."[95] The message is clear—*Plessy* played a role in defeating a budding interracial alliance in the South, but that failure was not inevitable before or even immediately after *Plessy*. While the resistance to the Populists from southern Democrats and the Supreme Court was formidable, the outcome was still hanging in the balance in 1896.

The Court's efforts to discredit the forces of reform only intensified their resolve. As one Populist author wrote, "I am aware that the people have heard from the Supreme Court on this subject. The Supreme Court will hear from the people in the near future."[96]

FIVE

The Election of 1896

I come to speak to you in defense of a cause as holy as
the cause of liberty—the cause of humanity.
—WILLIAM JENNINGS BRYAN

The shootout between the Populists and their constitutional foes
reached its climax during a presidential election that broke all
of the rules. A thirty-six-year-old former congressman, William
Jennings Bryan, was selected as the Democratic and Populist
nominee and bucked a century of precedent by campaigning personally for the job. He mounted this effort in the face of tough
opposition from supporters of President Cleveland and with
the burden of having two vice presidential running mates (one
from each party), which raised the prospect that he would win
but end up with a Republican vice president. Meanwhile, William McKinley, the Republican standard-bearer, put together a
massive fund-raising operation that would set the standard for all
future campaigns. And for the only time in American history, the
idea of packing the Supreme Court with partisans was debated in

a presidential election. The three parties were calling on voters to render a final verdict on the great constitutional question for this generation: Should the Populist reform project go forward?

Fusion or Independence?

The most important question about the 1896 election, at least for the purposes of this book, is, Why did the Populists lose? In every other generational contest, the rebels overwhelmed the old guard and implemented their program after winning a climactic election or series of elections. The Populist movement is the only exception, and its failure requires an explanation. And the only way to assess what went wrong is by looking closely at how Bryan was chosen as the Populist and Democratic nominee for president.

In 1895 and early 1896, Populist activists were consumed by a debate over whether to remain an independent third party or to combine with the Democrats.[1] Tom Watson led the middle-of-the-roaders, who contended that fusion with the Democrats would end the distinctive qualities of Populism and create a world where "we play Jonah while they play whale."[2] James Weaver took the opposite tack and argued that the 1892 and 1894 election results proved that the party could not win on its own. Weaver said, "I am a middle-of-the-road man, but I don't propose to lie down across of it so no one can get over me. Nothing grows in the middle of the road."[3] This basic disagreement was partly a reflection of the sectional fracture within Populist ranks. Watson did not support cooperating with Democrats at the national level because they were his sworn enemy throughout the South. In the Midwest, though, the Populists were loosely allied with the Democrats already and thus had no problem with making that bond permanent.

Fusionists and middle-of-the-roaders also disagreed about the message that the party should take into the general election. Weaver and his supporters thought that free silver was a winning issue and that the rest of the Populist platform should be downplayed.[4] In part, this concession was necessary to create an alliance with anti-Cleveland Democrats, who were unenthusiastic about the rest of the rural agenda.[5] Other leaders argued that currency reform was not especially important and that it would not appeal to urban Catholic voters, who were already uneasy with Populist candidates and their hostility toward immigrants.[6] Moreover, activists such as Henry Demarest Lloyd claimed that free silver was just a Trojan horse that would let silver-mining interests grab control of the party.[7]

In practical terms, this discussion boiled down to a decision about when the Populists should hold their national convention. The middle-of-the-roaders wanted to schedule the convention before the Democrats held theirs.[8] This would secure the party's autonomy and allow its candidate to pick off Democrats angered by whatever result emerged from their convention in Chicago. Fusionists, on the other hand, wanted the Populist convention delayed. Their hope was that the Democrats would select a silver candidate, which would stampede the Populist convention into nominating the same man a few weeks later. In a series of skirmishes that only hard-core fans of intrigue could love, the fusionists successfully stacked the relevant party committees and got their way.

While that fight was going on, the supporters of a marriage between Democrats and Populists already had a candidate in mind: Bryan. Born in 1860, he moved to Nebraska in 1887 and immediately became a power in local politics. He was elected to Congress in 1890 and served two terms—during which he sponsored the income tax struck down in *Pollock*—before running a losing Senate race in 1894. A common misconception about Bryan is that he was an unknown who won the presidential nomination with one fantastic speech. In fact, he spent most of 1895 and 1896 speaking around the country to Democratic activists and kept in touch with the fusionists.[9] Weaver even advised him of their scheme to postpone the Populist convention, writing in one letter: "We have had quite enough middle of the road nonsense, and some of us at least think it about time for the exhibition of a little synthetic force."[10] As a result, when Bryan arrived in Chicago, he could count on a bloc of supporters on the floor and on sympathy outside the hall.[11]

The leading obstacle to Bryan's nomination came from "Gold Democrats," who backed President Cleveland's policies, but they soon realized that they were outnumbered.[12] The president opposed Bryan's candidacy and told his supporters that "a cause worth fighting for is worth fighting for to the end."[13] Nevertheless, by 1896, Cleveland did not have much influence with the party faithful. A Gold Democrat describing the scene in Chicago said that for "the first time, I can understand the scenes of the French Revolution."[14] The conservative senator David Hill of New York, in a desperate plea to the delegates, said: "I am a Democrat, but I am not a revolutionist. My mission here today is to unite, not to divide—to build up, not to destroy."[15] Bryan dismissed these efforts and boasted that he would soon "walk down the aisle and put the gold standard delegation on the tip of my toe as they are being kicked out of the Convention."[16]

The triumphal moment, of course, was Bryan's "Cross of Gold" speech on behalf of a silver platform, which provided a memorable statement of the agrarian creed. Aided by a baritone voice that could reach an entire arena in an era before microphones, Bryan defended the role of farmers in society: "The great cities rest upon our broad and fertile prairies. Burn down your cities and leave our farms, and your cities will spring up again as if by magic; but destroy our farms, and the grass will grow in the streets of every city in the country."[17] He also lashed out at the "few financial magnates who, in a back room, corner the money of the world" and expressed the anger that activists felt about the resistance they had faced over the past few years from the president and from the Court: "We have petitioned, and our petitions have been scorned. We have entreated, and our entreaties have been disregarded. We have begged, and they have mocked when our calamity came. We beg no longer. We entreat no more. We petition no more. We defy them!"[18] He ended with this famous rallying cry: "Having behind us the producing masses of this nation and the world, supported by the commercial interests, the laboring interests, and the toilers everywhere, we will answer their demand for a gold standard by saying to them: You shall not press down upon the brow of labor this crown of thorns, you shall not crucify mankind upon a cross of gold!"[19] Though this speech did not guarantee Bryan's nomination (he did not win until the fifth ballot), it clearly played a big role in his selection.

To attract Populist support, the Democratic platform embraced some of their priorities. For example, the party criticized Cleveland's handling of the Pullman Strike, supported free silver, advocated limits on immigration, and endorsed increased federal regulation (though not outright ownership) of railroads and other industries.[20] With respect to the federal income tax, the platform attacked *Pollock* for rejecting "the uniform decisions of that court for nearly 100 years . . . We declare that it is the duty of the Congress to use all the Constitutional power which remains after the decision, or which may come from its reversal by the court as it may hereafter be constituted."[21] This statement led to the charge that Democrats supported "Court-packing."

The Democratic Party also attempted to placate Gold Democrats by choosing a conservative running mate for Bryan, but the faction that supported the president was not satisfied. Arthur

Sewell, the vice presidential nominee, was a businessman from New York who agreed with Bryan on nothing except free silver.[22] The Gold Democrats still left the hall and held their own rally to select a separate ticket.[23] In their platform, they said: "All good citizens of the republic are bound to repudiate [the Chicago platform] and exert every lawful means to insure the defeat of the candidates that represent these false doctrines."[24] They also maintained that "the Democratic party has survived many defeats, but could not survive a victory won in behalf of the doctrine and the policy proclaimed in its name at Chicago."[25]

A few weeks later, when the Populists held their convention in Saint Louis, open warfare broke out between the fusionists and the middle-of-the-roaders. Advocates of independence—Jacob Coxey and Ignatius Donnelly, among others—argued that the Populist nomination of Bryan would be "a surrender of the People's Party movement and the destruction of their present magnificent organization."[26] To derail this result, they attacked Sewell, Bryan's Democratic running mate, and convinced the delegates to nominate Tom Watson instead. Then they turned to the presidential nomination, hoping that Bryan would not accept a different Populist vice presidential candidate.[27] In fact, Bryan did write the convention chair stating that he would not run with Watson, but the chair (in an era before cable news) kept this from the delegates until after they had voted for Bryan.[28]

So fusion was achieved, but at a high cost. First, President Cleveland and what was left of his party machine actively opposed the national ticket, which was not helpful for Bryan. Second, the existence of two vice presidential candidates reinforced the sectional split within the Populist coalition. Indeed, Watson used many of his campaign speeches to attack Sewell rather than to praise Bryan.[29] This was emblematic of the alienation of the middle-of-the-road faction and its unenthusiastic support for the ticket. Third, Bryan's emphasis on the silver issue, the subject of the Cross of Gold speech, proved to be a mistake because it had no appeal beyond his rural base. In November, McKinley would win every significant city except for New Orleans.[30] Such a dreadful result was not surprising, since Populists generally thought that cities were part of the problem, not part of the solution, and they did little to reach out to unions or to the urban bosses that were critical in turning out the Democratic vote. All of these structural flaws contributed to Bryan's defeat.

To offset these disadvantages, Bryan embarked on a nationwide tour, during which he made six hundred speeches to an estimated five million people.[31] Today we are accustomed to direct campaigns, but it was then considered undignified for presidential candidates to ask for votes, which is why there are no general election speeches from Washington, Jefferson, Jackson, or Lincoln.[32] Bryan's decision to break with that long-standing practice was in keeping with the turbulent times, and his approach soon became the standard and enhanced the power of the president within the constitutional design—yet another example of how the necessities of political competition created new doctrines and traditions in the 1890s. The tactic also reinforced the popular character of Bryan's movement and created a vivid contrast with the Republican Party.

William McKinley and the Supreme Court

Conservatives were stunned by Bryan's nomination. Their resistance had brought reformers into control of a major party rather than burying them. The *New York Times* ran blazing headlines—"Bryan the Demagogue" and "Logical Candidate of the Party of Fantastic Ideas"—and contended that Bryan "must at any cost and by whatever means are most effective be beaten."[33] The *Philadelphia Press* editorialized that Bryan's "riotous platform is the concrete creed of the mob. It is rank Populism intensified and edged with hate and venom. It rests upon the four corner stones of organized Repudiation, deliberate Confiscation, chartered Communism, and enthroned Anarchy."[34] John Hay, who would serve as McKinley's secretary of state, told Henry Adams that "a good many worthy Republicans are scared blue . . . of the Boy Orator of the Platte . . . What if the Baby Demosthenes should get in with this programme: Free silver; abolition of Supreme Court; abolition of national banks; confiscation of railroads and telegraphs! Add to this such trifles as seeing Debs Attorney General."[35]

The Republican convention in Saint Louis (held before Bryan was nominated by the Populists) was a relatively placid affair:

the representatives selected William McKinley as the party nominee on the first ballot.[36] Much like Bryan, McKinley has an undeservedly poor reputation. Although he is often portrayed as nothing more than a tool of Mark Hanna, his wealthy campaign manager, McKinley was an adept politician who excelled at backroom deals and at reading public opinion.[37] Consider his famous "front-porch" campaign strategy in 1896. McKinley knew that he could not match Bryan on the stump and that the traditional view that candidates should not speak for themselves was appealing to many voters.[38] At the same time, he could not just let Bryan monopolize the public stage. His solution to this dilemma was clever. Instead of going to the people, he brought the people to him. Hundreds of thousands of supporters made a pilgrimage to McKinley's home in Ohio, where he greeted them with a speech from his porch.[39] The Republicans also countered Bryan by sending the police commissioner of New York, Theodore Roosevelt, to speak in towns that Bryan had just visited. Roosevelt responded with enthusiasm, convinced that "if Bryan wins, we have before us some years of social misery, not markedly different from that of any South American republic."[40]

Whereas McKinley was simply responding to Bryan's pioneering campaign style, he matched the challenger's creativity when it came to campaign organization. Mark Hanna, who thought that the "Chicago convention from beginning to end was in the hands of a clique of radicals and revolutionists," used the fear of a Democratic win to put together the first massive

President William McKinley.
Library of Congress.

fund-raising machine.[41] He drew up a schedule of recommended "assessments" for every major corporation and put that money to work, employing a blizzard of paid volunteers, handing out leaflets, and planting essays in the press to support McKinley.[42] Bryan was unable to match this flood of money and was outspent by about ten to one during the campaign. Once again, the process of mutual transformation was forcing each side in this generational fight to launch ever more powerful responses—legal or political—to match what the other was doing.

Rather than give a blow-by-blow account of the presidential campaign, I want to focus on the leading constitutional question between Bryan and McKinley: the plank of the Democratic/ Populist platform that criticized *Pollock* and, because it expressly mentioned "the court as it may hereafter be constituted," was read as a pledge to pack the Supreme Court with radicals. There are two famous examples of Court-packing in U.S. history. One was Franklin D. Roosevelt's unsuccessful effort to increase the membership of the Court in 1937. The other was Andrew Jackson's success in expanding the number of Justices from seven to nine in 1837.[43] Most lawyers know about the first case; the second is not so well known but did serve as a precedent for anyone who wanted to take the Court-packing route in the 1890s.

Conservatives saw the *Pollock* plank as a "smoking gun" indicating that Bryan was bent on destroying the Constitution. Gold Democrats argued, for instance, that Bryan "assails the independence of the judiciary by a covert threat to reorganize the courts whenever their decisions contravene the decree of the party caucus."[44] In their view, the Supreme Court's "independence and authority to interpret the law of the land without fear or favor must be maintained. We condemn all efforts to degrade that tribunal or impair the confidence and respect which it has deservedly held."[45] The Gold Democratic vice presidential nominee added that Bryan "would wipe virtually out of existence that Supreme Court which interprets the law, forgetting that our ancestors in England fought for hundreds of years to obtain a tribunal of justice which was free from executive control."[46]

Pamphleteers and journalists who backed McKinley made similar criticisms. One campaign book attacked the Democrats as "zealots" who "propose among their early doings to reorganize the Supreme Court of the United States."[47] Another said that it "is not the fact that the Chicago platform criticized the judiciary that has brought down our condemnation, but it is the unwisdom and the un-Americanism of their implied threat to reconstruct the Supreme Court for partisan purposes."[48] *Harper's Weekly* wrote that "Mr. BRYAN's government would destroy that safeguard by packing the Supreme Court with judges who would agree with the Constitutional views of the legislative branch if that branch happened to be in the hands of the Populists."[49] Not to be outdone, the *New York Times* told its readers that Bryan wanted "a packed Supreme Court."[50] And another conservative lawyer wrote: "There are two places in this country where all men are absolutely equal: One is the ballot-box and the other is the Supreme Court. Bryan proposes to abolish the Supreme Court and make it the creature of the party caucus whenever a new Congress comes in."[51]

Republicans also pounced on this issue, but their argument offered a more sophisticated synthesis of constitutional law. In the party campaign manual, the Republicans held that from "the days of *Marbury v. Madison* to those of the income-tax cases, there have been many criticisms of the opinions of the Supreme Court, but the platform at Chicago is the first party assault upon the constitutional tenure of the Justices."[52] This statement is fascinating because it demonstrates that the rediscovery of *Marbury* now reached well beyond the Court. What began as clever rhetoric by Joseph H. Choate to talk the Justices into rejecting their own precedent on direct taxes was now becoming part of mainstream political discourse. The Populists responded by attacking Chief Justice Marshall, with one writing in the *Ameri-*

can Law Review that *Marbury* was a "usurpation by the Federal courts of the legislative power" and could not justify *Pollock.*[53]

The view that Bryan was going to pack the Court was depicted by a cartoon on the cover of *Harper's Weekly* dated September 12, 1896, entitled "A Forecast of the Consequence of a Popocratic Victory to the Supreme Court of the United States."[54] In it, the Court sits under the Jolly Roger and a "fifty-cent bunco dollar" made of silver. The Constitution lies trampled on the ground, and the four busts above the bench depict Charles Guiteau, the assassin of President James Garfield, and three of the anarchists convicted in the bloody Haymarket Riot of 1886.[55] The Justices include Governor Altgeld as Chief Justice (in the center); "Pitchfork" Ben Tillman, the free-silver governor of South Carolina; Eugene Debs (wearing the "King Debs" crown); and Jacob Coxey (wearing a helmet of Coxey's Army). The message was clear: Bryan's Court would validate a scary agenda that should be rejected at the polls.

Bryan hit back at the Court-packing charges in a major speech at Madison Square Garden. He explained that his "opponents endeavored to make it appear that the income tax plank of our platform assailed the Supreme Court. This criticism was entirely without foundation. The platform commended the income tax, and suggested the possibility that the court might hereafter reverse its decision and return to the earlier precedents."[56] After all, he continued, "a future court has a right to declare a similar income tax law constitutional. Even the present members of the

NEW YORK, SATURDAY, SEPTEMBER 12, 1896.

ON A POPULISTIC BASIS.
A FORECAST OF THE CONSEQUENCE OF A DEMOCRATIC VICTORY TO THE SUPREME COURT OF THE UNITED STATES.

Harper's Weekly cover of September 12, 1896. Library of Congress.

court have a right to change their opinions on this subject as judges have in the past changed their opinions."[57] In another speech, Bryan made a legal realist argument: The "Supreme court changes from time to time. Judges die or resign, and new judges take their places. Is it not possible, my friends, that future judges may adhere to the precedents of a hundred years, instead of adhering to a decision rendered by a majority of one?"[58]

Bryan's statements about the Court can be interpreted in at least two ways. He may have been saying that he would choose Justices who disagreed with *Pollock* and its constitutional philosophy. Making choices on the basis of political philosophy is perfectly normal presidential behavior and not the same as picking party hacks or increasing the size of the Court, as Bryan's critics charged. Alternatively, he may have thought that a victory at the polls would force the Justices into a "switch-in-time," by which I mean that they would retract their resistance and embrace the reform agenda.[59] The term "switch-in-time" is often used to describe what happened after President Roosevelt's landslide victory in 1936 (and his actual threat to pack the bench), when at least some of the Justices read the election returns as an endorsement of the New Deal and started adjusting doctrine accordingly.[60] But what lesson would the Court draw if Bryan lost? That is the critical question that constitutional theory ignores and that chapter 6 addresses.

What stands out about the 1896 debate about Court-packing is the willingness of both sides to engage the electorate in defining the constitutional stakes. The cycle of escalation begun by President Cleveland's decision to oppose the Populists in 1893 had culminated just three years later in a sharp ideological polarization that forced the American people to consider first principles anew, up to and including the role of the Supreme Court. The voters now gave their answer.

Realignment and the Future

Well into September, most observers thought that Bryan held the lead. On election day, however, his disadvantages caught up with him. With a voter turnout that reached an astounding 80 percent, the Republican Party retained control of Congress, and William McKinley carried the country by a decisive margin.[61] The Republican victory was by 600,000 votes out of 13,900,000, and Bryan lost in the Electoral College by 271 to 176.[62] More important, McKinley received a majority of the popular vote (51 percent), which no presidential candidate had done since Ulysses S. Grant in 1872.[63] This result was also significant (and ominous for African Americans) because it showed that Republicans did not need the South to win, which undermined their incentive to fight for African American suffrage against the future encroachments of the white establishment there.[64]

Even though definite proof was lacking at the time, the evidence would grow that "the switching voters were not coerced into voting for McKinley; they were converted."[65] In other words, the traumatic events that preceded the 1896 election branded a political identity on a new generational cohort that would dominate the constitutional cycle until the Great Depression. That group of voters continued to refer back to the dark days of the 1890s in future elections and to vote in a similar way, much as the Democrats and Whigs did following the 1830s and the Republicans and Democrats did following the 1860s. This gut-level association and the partisan loyalties created by it was reinforced by the Democrats' decision to nominate Bryan for president again in 1900 and 1908, which let Republicans, much to their delight, run the 1896 campaign over and over.[66]

Conservatives breathed a sigh of relief at McKinley's triumph. *The Nation* exulted because the country had "escaped from . . . an immense danger, the danger of having our currency adulterated and our form of government changed, and a band of ignoramuses and Anarchists put at the head of what remained of the great American republic."[67] Principled resistance (at least from a conservative point of view) had succeeded. Nevertheless, the Populists still posed a threat, and over the next four years political and legal elites took additional steps to codify the mandate of 1896 and to ensure that the spirit of reform would not make a comeback. The tragedy of William Jennings Bryan was about to unfold.

SIX

A New Constitutional Regime

If, then, the "due process of law" required by the Fourteenth
Amendment does not allow a state to take private property
without just compensation, but does allow the life or liberty of
the citizen to be taken in a mode that is repugnant to the settled
usages and the modes of proceeding authorized at the time the
Constitution was adopted and which was expressly forbidden by
the national Bill of Rights, it would seem that the protection
of private property is of more consequence than the
protection of the life and liberty of the citizen.
—John Marshall Harlan

Victorious armies do not call off their pursuit when the enemy's lines break, and the same principle applies to politicians
and lawyers engaged in generational conflict. Like many "temporary" emergency measures, the extraordinary actions taken
against the Populists before the 1896 election became constitutional fixtures. Over the next few years, the Justices extended
those precedents and in so doing bridged the divide in Fourteenth Amendment doctrine concerning property and contract
rights, racial discrimination, and incorporation. The result of
this backlash was a legal regime that lasted, with just a few exceptions, until the middle of the twentieth century.

A Green Light for Conservatives

The most important takeaway from the events of the 1890s is that steps taken to resist an intense popular mobilization for constitutional change do not merely restate existing law but actually change the law in response to the goals and arguments of reformers. A survey of the doctrine in 1896 confirms this point. The Populist Party strongly supported a federal income tax. After *Pollock*, advocates of the tax faced major new constitutional hurdles. Southern Populists were keen on racial cooperation and on the protection of African American rights (at least up to a point). After *Plessy*, racial segregation was constitutionally protected. Agrarian activists maintained that the Commerce Clause supported nationalization and putting businesses under more stringent state law supervision. Instead, the clause was read to give the president and the courts broad power to prohibit strikes, and the Court held that the states faced substantive Fourteenth Amendment limits on their ability to regulate railroad rates. Accordingly, in almost every area that Bryan and his supporters cared about, the law was changed between 1894 and 1896 to block and subvert their hopes. As I explained in chapter 1, these doctrinal changes were not related to the original understanding of the Fourteenth Amendment or to the gradual and logically consistent evolution of case law.

A violent recoil occurs at almost every inflection point between constitutional generations, but that snapback is almost always temporary; either it is quickly forgotten, or it becomes an example of what the law will no longer tolerate. For instance, the British enacted several repressive statutes and taxes to crush colonial unrest in the 1760s and 1770s, but the Revolution overthrew those measures. The Alien and Sedition Act of 1798 was intended to criminalize political criticism of the Federalists, but it lapsed after Jefferson was elected in 1800.[1] According to *Dred Scott*, slavery could not be banned from the territories and African Americans could never be citizens, but the Thirteenth and Fourteenth Amendments repudiated that decision.

But if the establishment had prevailed in these struggles the way it did in the 1890s, the long-term impact of this resistance would have been far greater. The problem is that there is no automatic "constitutional sunset" that can keep a judicial precedent established under abnormal conditions from expanding when normalcy is restored.[2] It is possible, of course, for the Court to distinguish a prior decision—as it did with *Pollock* in the *Springer* case, which upheld the wartime income tax. Much of the time, though, courts treat opinions as authoritative and apply them without regard to the political context in which they were issued. What this means is that the law can get stuck with broad and haphazard preemptive opinions long after the political threat that created them passes. And these cases then form a new interpretive baseline or set of first principles for judges and lawyers.

The legacy of successful constitutional resistance is not just a question of formalism and precedent, for courts can also read an election victory by their generational partners as an endorsement of their opinions in controversial cases. This is the opposite of a switch-in-time. Instead of folding, as the Justices can do when the people decisively reject the Court's actions, the Justices took McKinley's victory as a sign that they could expand on the principles that they had articulated right before the election. A switch-in-time and what I will call a "green light" both involve a dramatic shift in the law even though the membership of the Court stays the same.[3] Both are also political explanations for the Justices' opinions that are disconnected from the reasoning in the cases. It should thus come as no surprise that Bryan's defeat and the Court's reaction led Finley Peter Dunne, the noted satirist, to comment, "The Supreme Court follows the election returns."[4] In this instance, the election returns supported a dramatic move away from Bryan's ideas.

The Justices were not starting from scratch after the Republican sweep in 1896. They were already divided on the meaning of the Fourteenth Amendment. What the Populist failure did, however, was alter the balance within the Court in favor of those who wanted more protection for property and contract rights, less protection for civil liberties, and greater deference to the states on racial questions. In the end, Bryan's crusade was like a social call by Typhoid Mary—well intentioned but devastating.

The Elevation of Property and Contract Rights

That the shock wave from McKinley's victory had reached the Court is evident in two cases handed down just a few days before the new president's inauguration. In each of the opinions, the Justices held without dissent that the Fourteenth Amendment applied new limits to state regulatory authority. Their unanimity was significant because it meant that the debate over property and contract rights that had raged since *Slaughter-House* was over, and the fight was turning to the breadth of constitutional protection afforded to these common-law rights and the role that *Slaughter-House* should play now that its core holding was no more. The switch-in-time analogy can be invoked again: these cases are structurally similar to the Commerce Clause cases issued in the aftermath of the New Deal, such as *United States v. Darby* and *Wickard v. Fillburn*, in which the Justices were unanimous in their broad view of the commerce power and which basically ended the debate about the scope of that provision.[5]

In *Chicago, Burlington, and Quincy Railroad Co. v. Chicago*, the first of the two cases issued before the inaugural, the Court held that the Due Process Clause of the Fourteenth Amendment applied the Takings Clause to the states.[6] *Chicago* involved an exercise of eminent domain by the city to widen a street, which led a property owner to complain that its compensation was inadequate. Declaring that the "protection of the rights of property has been regarded as a vital principle of republican institutions," the Court explained that "a judgment of a state court . . . whereby private property is taken for the state or under its direction for public use, without compensation made or secured to the owner is . . . wanting in the due process of law required by the fourteenth amendment."[7] It would be wrong to say that this decision was particularly significant, for the Takings Clause was rarely invoked against state action afterwards.[8] In addition, the *Chicago* opinion basically followed the reasoning in the 1894 *Reagan* case, in which the Court applied takings principles to the states through an equal protection theory—an approach consistent with statements in previous decisions that the substantive portions of the Bill of Rights should be incorporated.

Far more significant was the *Allgeyer v. Louisiana* decision, issued on the same day as *Chicago*. In it the Court held that the Fourteenth Amendment also protected a "liberty of contract." Justice Rufus Peckham, who wrote the *Allgeyer* opinion and extended that holding eight years later in *Lochner*, was the leading author of the McKinley green-light decisions. *Allgeyer* was a bland case about a Louisiana statute that regulated marine insurance contracts, but what Peckham said was not dull at all. He said that the liberty mentioned in the Due Process Clause of the Fourteenth Amendment meant the right "of the citizen to be free in the enjoyment of all his faculties; to be free to use them in all lawful ways; to live and work where he will; to earn his livelihood by any lawful calling; to pursue any livelihood or avocation; and for that purpose to enter into all contracts which may be proper."[9]

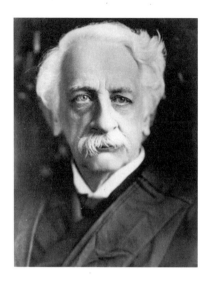

Justice Rufus Peckham, author of
*Allgeyer v. Louisiana, Maxwell v.
Dow,* and *Lochner v. New York.* The
Oyez Project, www.oyez.org.

The Court also said that this new constitutional right was open ended: whereas states had a police power to regulate on behalf of the health and welfare of their citizens, "when and how far such power may be legitimately exercised with regard to these subjects must be left for determination to each case as it arises."[10] This language was crucial because it directly contradicted the Court's holding in *Slaughter-House* that the Fourteenth Amendment did not protect common-law rights, especially the right "to pursue any livelihood or avocation," such as being a butcher. *Allgeyer* did not explicitly say that *Slaughter-House* was overruled, but that was the obvious implication of the decision.[11] The instability created by the Populist challenge, which toppled long-standing precedent on the Direct Tax Clauses, the Commerce Clause, and the way presidential campaigns were conducted, had claimed another victim. Yet the shell of *Slaughter-House* remained, and the Justices soon found something new to say about it.

Allgeyer was the cornerstone of a new approach that gave courts greater latitude than before to review the substance of state law regulation on economic matters. To buttress the legitimacy of this change and of the other interpretive innovations that expanded judicial review during the 1890s, the bar launched a concerted effort to make *Marbury* untouchable. The process of establishing Marshall's sainthood, which started with *Pollock* and continued during the 1896 race, accelerated after Bryan was beaten. *Marbury* was now lauded as a "bulwark of liberty and civilization, towering above all others erected by the Anglo-Saxon race."[12] The American Bar Association promoted "John Marshall Day" in 1901 to celebrate the centennial of his appointment to the Court; judges and politicians participated in ceremonies across the country.[13] Chief Justice Melville Fuller, the author of *Pollock*, even spoke before a joint session of Congress on Marshall Day.[14] And Justice George Shiras, another member of the *Pollock* majority, urged a friend to establish "a consensus of opinion concerning Marshall on the part of eminent lawyers in all parts of the country."[15] This request indicates a lack of consensus about his importance (or about *Marbury*) until this time. Indeed, the president of the Georgia Bar Association commented that too many people were trying to revive the "frightful ghost of Marshallism."[16] Just as Bryan's failure undid *Slaughter-House*, it also turned *Marbury* into a powerhouse.[17]

The Triumph of White Supremacy

While the Justices were busy expanding federal constitutional protection for property and contract rights, southern Democrats eager to reinforce Jim Crow also saw the 1896 election as a green light.[18] Populists in the South already had an uneasy relationship with the national party because of their resistance to fusion, and Bryan's defeat sent the southern membership of the party into a death spiral.[19] The consolidation of the conservative triumph proceeded with the rapid expansion of segregation from railroads to nearly all aspects of life. There was some opposition by Populists in state legislatures and in lawsuits challenging school segregation.[20] But once these activists were removed as a vital political force, nothing stood in the way of Jim Crow's march across the South.[21]

Democratic plans to end voting by African Americans and by poor whites generated a more intense battle.[22] In the six years following Bryan's 1896 defeat, most southern states implemented a poll tax, a grandfather clause, the all-white primary, and a literacy test, thereby eliminating any experiments with interracial cooperation.[23] These suffrage "reforms" had an immediate and devastating impact. In Louisiana the number of registered African American voters fell from 130,334 in 1896 to 5,320 by 1900.[24] In Alabama the total fell from 181,471 to 3,000 after a new state constitution took effect in 1901. Virginia and North Carolina were even more efficient, taking the number of African American voters down to zero! The number of white voters (those who could afford the poll tax) also declined precipitously in these states after 1900.[25] Instead of beating or joining the Populist coalition, the southern Democratic establishment just erased it.

This transformation of state constitutional law, which amounted to the greatest rollback of democracy in U.S. history, was enacted by a relatively narrow margin. In Alabama and North Carolina the referenda to ratify these changes passed only because African Americans were excluded from a vote that they were eligible for (on whether they should keep voting) or else were counted as voting for the new constitutions even though they did not.[26] In a study of the Alabama vote in the 1920s the authors concluded that the "absent colored voters . . . voted for their own disenfranchisement," which could only have been the product of massive fraud.[27] Naturally, the Populists fought hard against these constitutional proposals, whose ratification would sound the death knell for their movement. Tom Watson and Marion Butler objected to these suffrage restrictions on the ground that "a man who fought the battles of his country, and paid the taxes of his government, should have a vote in the choosing of rulers and the making of laws."[28] When this protest failed, African Americans in Alabama brought a Fifteenth Amendment claim to the Supreme Court and sought an injunction ordering the state to register them.

The opinion in *Giles v. Harris* (1903) upholding the new suffrage limits in Alabama is described by Richard H. Pildes as "probably the most momentous ignored decision in the history of the Supreme Court."[29] *Giles* stands alongside *Chicago*, *Allgeyer*, and *Maxwell v. Dow* as one of the transformative cases that elaborated the principles flowing from the mandate against Bryan. The state's lawyer did not mince words about the Alabama constitutional amendments: they would bar "many whites" and "the mass of the negro population" from voting.[30] Justice Oliver Wendell Holmes Jr., in his opinion, answered that it "seems to us impossible to grant the . . . relief which is asked."[31] He explained that courts were powerless to disturb the constitutional settlement created by the Populist defeat. The suit in *Giles* claimed "that the great mass of the white population intends to keep the blacks from voting . . . Unless we are prepared to supervise the voting in that state by officers of the court, it seems to us that all the plaintiff could get from equity would be an empty form . . . [because] relief from a great political wrong, if done, as alleged, by the people of a state and the state itself, must be given by them or by the legislative and political department of the government of the United States."[32]

This passage is either the most cowardly or the most realistic in Supreme Court history. In essence, Holmes was saying that the Fifteenth Amendment could not be enforced because too many white southerners were determined to prevent that from happening. If this reading is correct, then *Giles* was simply validating mob rule. Another way of looking at the decision, however, is to accept that the Justices recognized that the

Justice Oliver Wendell Holmes Jr., author of *Giles v. Harris.* Library of Congress. Photo by Louis Fabian Bachrach, circa 1930.

Constitution had been effectively amended by the generational battle of the 1890s. This view is suggested by the Court's reference to the political branches, for neither Congress nor President Theodore Roosevelt took up *Giles*'s invitation to roll back the South's nullification of the Fifteenth Amendment.[33] When all of the relevant governing institutions are in accord, as they were here, about an informal revision of the Constitution, the Justices usually respond by developing a new doctrinal test or by recasting their precedents to accommodate the change. *Giles* was simply more honest (and thus more jarring) because the Justices refused to paper over the rupture created by Bryan's failure, in part because there was no artful way to explain the collapse of suffrage.[34] By 1904 the Jim Crow republic was firmly in place and would continue to impose its cruelty until the generation led by Martin Luther King Jr. came along in the 1960s.

This story about race has a sad postscript. Embittered by defeat, many southern Populists concluded that their alliance with African Americans was to blame for their failure. In part because of their displaced anger but also because embracing white supremacy was the only way to prosper politically, many Populist leaders became racist demagogues in the early part of the twentieth century. One of the most reactionary of these politicians was none other than Tom Watson, who became a U.S. senator from Georgia in 1920 by making the kinds of racist and anti-Semitic appeals that he had condemned in his youth.[35]

Slaughter-House and Incorporation

The final issue for which McKinley's green light proved crucial was the application of the Bill of Rights to the states. In *Maxwell*, the Court was presented with a claim that the conviction of a criminal defendant in Utah by an eight-member jury (instead of the usual twelve) violated the Sixth Amendment as incorporated by the Fourteenth Amendment.[36] Justice Peckham rejected this claim in part by citing recent cases holding that the procedural protections of the Bill of Rights should not be extended. In this sense, there was nothing remarkable about *Maxwell*.[37]

As we saw in chapter 1, however, *Maxwell* broke new ground with its reinterpretation of *Slaughter-House* as a decision that was hostile to incorporation. In the aftermath of *Allgeyer*, the Justices had a hard time understanding what *Slaughter-House* meant. For instance, Justice Peckham wrote that if *Maxwell*'s incorporation claim prevailed, then *Slaughter-House* would have to be over-ruled.[38] But this was not true, since the holding of *Slaughter-House* was about contract and property rights, not about juries. More important, *Allgeyer* did overrule *Slaughter-House* in prac-tice. The problem was that the Justices could not openly admit that they had overruled the first decision interpreting the Four-teenth Amendment—that would be too embarrassing. Indeed, in none of the landmark cases during the 1890s, even *Pollock*, did the Court say that it was overruling precedent.

Although *Slaughter-House* could not be overruled, it could be given a new reading. In *Maxwell*, the Court accomplished this by spending four pages discussing the case before concluding that it stood for the idea that the entire Bill of Rights—substantive and procedural—was not included among the national privi-leges or immunities protected by the Fourteenth Amendment. The Court explained: "We have made this extended reference to the case because of its great importance, the thoroughness of the treatment of the subject, and the great ability displayed by the author of the opinion . . . The opinion upon the matters actually involved and maintained by the judgment in the case has never been doubted or overruled by any judgment of this court."[39] This passage was a legal fiction. *Maxwell*'s dictum was not con-sistent with what *Slaughter-House* held, but Justice Peckham's claim in *Maxwell* was consistent with the shift in elite attitudes on incorporation and property rights during the 1890s. The Pullman Strike, *Debs,* and the fear of radicalism all contributed to a climate in which, as Justice Harlan stated in his dissent, "the protection of private property is of more consequence than the protection of the life and liberty of the citizen."[40] Harlan's statement is a fairly concise expression of the constitutional backlash against the Populists.

Furthermore, the Court's analysis was consistent with the Jim Crow system and the retreat of voting rights. This is an important point. A real challenge to the oppression in the South could not succeed without federal protection of free speech and other fundamental rights for those who sought to criticize segregation. Indeed, the Court recognized this in cases during the 1960s, when state officials targeted civil rights activists.[41] So by rejecting incorporation beyond the Takings Clause, the Justices were (consciously or not) shoring up *Plessy* and *Giles.* We could also say that the rollback of the Fifteenth Amendment, which involved a constitutional right against state action, matched the corresponding diminution of support for extending other textual rights.

A final case that shed light on incorporation was *Downes v. Bidwell,* which addressed the application of the Constitution to territories acquired by the United States during the Spanish-American War.[42] When Bryan and McKinley faced off in their 1900 rematch, the main campaign issue was imperialism and the morality of the Spanish-American War. Bryan argued that becoming a colonial power would corrupt American democracy by requiring the maintenance of a large standing army. The "question," he said, "is not what we can do, but what we *ought* to do."[43] Theodore Roosevelt, an ardent expansionist and McKinley's new vice presidential running mate, took on this claim in speeches around the country. He told a friend that Bryan was gathering all "the lunatics, all the idiots, all the knaves, all the cowards, and all the honest people who are slow-witted" under his banner.[44] The result in 1900 was more lopsided than in 1896, with McKinley winning by more than 750,000 votes and carrying the Electoral College by 292 to 155.[45]

This victory gave the Court another green light, but this time it used the mandate to uphold broad congressional discretion in governing the new conquests. Although its response showed yet again that doctrine in these years was largely a reaction against whatever Bryan wanted or whatever would help his supporters, in this case there was a twist. The issue of whether the Constitution should extend to the territories (and thereby limit congressional discretion) was similar to the issue of incorporation. For both, the issue was whether constitutional rights or provisions should be expanded to new political units (the states or the territories). And the Court's rejection, in a series of cases, of jury trials and other constitutional rights in the Philippines was partly prompted by a desire to curb dissent, as were some of its decisions with respect to the Populists. In fact, after the Spanish-American War, the United States met a serious revolt in the Philippines with a harsh response that was not at all consistent with the Cruel and Unusual Punishments Clause.[46] Both abroad and at home, the Bill of Rights was on the defensive by 1900.

The irony of the 1890s is that one of the most impressive grass-roots movements in American history created one of the most repressive regimes in American history. Voting rights were stripped away from millions of people. Segregation was now the law of the land. Labor leaders were threatened with prison if they went on strike. The only exception to this trend came during the Progressive Era, especially in the second decade of the twentieth century. What looking at that period reveals, however, is that William Jennings Bryan continued to cast a long constitutional shadow.

SEVEN

The Progressive Correction

> The prime problem of our nation is to get the right type of good
> citizenship, and to get it, we must have progress, and our public
> men must be genuinely progressive.
> —THEODORE ROOSEVELT

The reforms of the Progressive Era seem to contradict the constitutional influence of the Populist failure, but in fact they confirm its importance. Richard Hofstadter asked in the 1950s how "a movement whose program was in the long run so generally successful [could] be identified with such a final and disastrous defeat for the class it was supposed to represent."[1] In other words, the argument that Bryan's defeat was a catastrophic setback cannot be correct, because Theodore Roosevelt and Woodrow Wilson put many Populist policies into law. A closer look at Progressivism, however, leads to a different conclusion. First, the legal principles introduced during the 1890s remained largely in place. Second, the few changes that were made occurred after 1908, when Bryan lost his last presidential race to William Howard Taft.[2] Once the specter of Bryan was removed, Republicans felt free to relax their resistance to reform, and to curb some of the excesses generated by the generational struggle. Accordingly, the Progressives are best understood as the backlash against the Populist backlash.

The Rough Rider Reconsidered

The spirit of reform that took hold after President McKinley's assassination in 1901 is an elusive target for legal commentators. Between 1913 and 1920, four constitutional amendments were ratified, which makes the Progressive Era the most textually important one other than the Founding and Reconstruction.[3] The Sixteenth Amendment, ratified in 1913, overruled *Pollock* and restored Congress's unfettered power to tax income. In the same year, the Seventeenth Amendment was ratified; the country thereby adopted the Populist proposal for the direct election of senators. After the First World War, the Eighteenth Amendment launched the ill-fated Prohibition experiment, and a year later, the Nineteenth Amendment gave full voting rights to women.

Nevertheless, the Progressive movement does not look like the other popular mobilizations for constitutional change that are discussed in this book as part of the generational cycle. Instead, Progressivism was an elite affair that drew its support mainly from professionals, who, not surprisingly, were enthusiastic about technocratic solutions to public policy questions.[4] It is difficult to find a popular groundswell for Progressive policies except in the 1912 election, when Roosevelt and Wilson carried a large majority of the vote in the three-way race with President Taft. With Warren Harding's win in 1920, the conservative wing of the Republican Party reasserted itself, and the trends of the prior decade were thrown into reverse until the Great Depression.

To understand the relationship between the Progressives and the Populists, the best place to start is with the wide gap between the myth and the reality of Theodore Roosevelt. He was without doubt a great president. The first to make America a major player on the diplomatic stage, he enhanced the power of the executive branch through his unilateral conduct of foreign affairs.[5] He was also the first modern president to use the media to sell his policy program, for he took full advantage of what he called the "bully pulpit" to make news. In domestic policy, though, Roosevelt was a moderate who refused to challenge the constitutional settlement of the 1890s. Indeed, he was always a rabid opponent of the Populists and, if anything, adopted a more reactionary view of them in 1896 and 1900 than McKinley did. People often confuse the Roosevelt of 1912, who ran for president on a third-party ticket that embraced a radical agenda, with the Roosevelt who as president trimmed his sails because he led a diverse Republican Party.[6]

Proof of Roosevelt's acquiescence in the status quo comes from the fact that constitutional doctrine in 1908, the last year

President Theodore Roosevelt.
Library of Congress.

of his administration, was virtually the same as when McKinley took office in 1897. The income tax was still considered a direct federal tax that had to be apportioned among the states, although there were growing calls among Republicans to pass a constitutional amendment that would repudiate that interpretation.[7] The Justices did decline to extend *Pollock* in 1900 by holding that inheritance taxes were not direct for constitutional purposes, but that was not a dramatic change.[8] Meanwhile, Jim Crow was flourishing in the South and reached a new level of intensity in the second decade of the century when President Wilson, who had been raised in Virginia, segregated the entire federal workforce.[9] The liberty of contract continued to show up in decisions such as *Lochner*, which struck down a New York law that established a maximum-hour limit for bakers, and *Adair v.*

United States, which invalidated a federal statute that prohibited railroads from requiring their employees to shun unions.[10] And the Court continued to reject the incorporation of the Bill of Rights, stating that the privileges or immunities issue decided in *Maxwell* was "no longer open in this court."[11]

Roosevelt's domestic policies were different from those of his predecessors, but they were either symbolic distractions or carefully designed to respect the constitutional scheme. For instance, Roosevelt's role as an honest broker during the coal strike of 1902 was rather different from Grover Cleveland's one-sided stance during the Pullman Strike.[12] Roosevelt's position certainly set a positive precedent for labor, but it was an act of balance and moderation, not a robust critique of current dogma. Likewise, Roosevelt brought a major antitrust suit against a railroad, but he left most of the trusts alone and selected a railroad as his target precisely because of *E. C. Knight*'s distinction between manufacturing and commerce: railroads were the paradigmatic commercial business.[13] Although the Court upheld this action in *Northern Securities Co. v. United States*, four Justices concluded that the Sherman Act did not apply, and the majority could not agree on a single opinion.[14] Furthermore, Roosevelt's major legislative achievements, such as the Hepburn Act, on railroad rate regulation, and the Pure Food and Drug Acts, on food safety, were crafted to meet his main criterion for success: "the one thing I do not want is to have a law passed and then declared unconstitutional."[15]

The point is that President Roosevelt's accomplishments were considerable but did not strike at the constitutional baseline set up by the 1896 election. Style more than substance characterized the succession from McKinley to Roosevelt.[16] Yet the Progressives cannot be entirely dismissed as a creative force, for some constitutional priorities did shift after 1908.

A Second-Order Backlash

The Taft administration's liveliness contrasted sharply with the constitutional caution that defined Roosevelt's tenure.[17] This may seem counterintuitive given Taft's conservative reputation, but consider the results. He proposed the Sixteenth Amendment and convinced Congress to send it along to the states for ratification (more on that later).[18] The liberty of contract went into hibernation and remained dormant throughout the next decade as the Justices became far more reluctant to invalidate laws using that doctrine.[19] Finally, President Taft brought many more antitrust prosecutions than Roosevelt did, and the Court responded by broadening the Sherman Act to apply to companies engaged in activities that went well beyond the narrow definition of commerce in *E. C. Knight*.[20] Indeed, in *Standard Oil Co. of New Jersey v. United States*, the Court broke up John D. Rockefeller's trust and said that the rationale in *E. C. Knight* was "unsound" and no longer valid.[21]

These changes were matched by a series of political upheavals that broke the power of the conservative leadership in Congress. In the House of Representatives, a bipartisan group of rebels deposed Joseph Cannon, the Republican Speaker famed for his autocratic grip on the chamber.[22] And over in the Senate, a similar revolt challenged the authority of Nelson Aldrich, often called the "Manager of the United States," who opposed liberal reform.[23] These divisions within Republican ranks opened the door for Democrats to gain control of the House in 1910, in their first victory of that magnitude since 1892.[24] Indeed, Bryan explained in 1910 that the "Republican Party is passing through the same crisis that the Democratic Party went through in 1896."[25] The key question is, Why did these constitutional and political changes occur at this time?

The popular answer is that the Panic of 1907 undermined support for conservative principles, but another explanation is that after the 1908 election Bryan was no longer a presidential threat and thus no longer united his opponents. One of the most striking facts about the Progressive leaders is that they all opposed Bryan in the 1890s. Louis Brandeis refused to support Bryan in 1896, and Woodrow Wilson voted for the Gold Democrats, telling a friend years later that the problem with Bryan was that "the man has no brains. It is a great pity that a man with his power of leadership should have no mental rudder."[26] They were joined in their skepticism by Lincoln Steffens, the muckraking journalist;

William Allen White, a reformer who made his name with an attack on Populism called "What's the Matter with Kansas?"; and George Norris, who became a leading liberal senator during the New Deal.[27] All of these reformers were inclined toward Populist policies, but they held that instinct at bay because, as the socialist author Jack London explained, even he would vote for McKinley if that was necessary to stop Bryan.[28] As another observer put it, "Bryan, Altgeld, and Debs seemed like the Dantons, Robespierres, and Marats of the coming upheaval. Hence there was a disposition among the middle classes to put aside their own discontents and grievances until the time should come when it seemed safe to air them."[29] It was finally safe in 1909.

Although Roosevelt was the most prominent example of a Progressive who pulled his punches while Bryan remained on the scene, the more intriguing case is William McKinley himself. Prior to 1896, McKinley forged a progressive record as a member of Congress and as the governor of Ohio. For instance, he backed women's suffrage and the direct election of senators well before either became part of the Constitution.[30] Neither of these causes went anywhere during his tenure, however, because the desire to keep Bryan out overwhelmed all other impulses. McKinley could have responded by offering the Populists carrots rather than sticks. But he accepted Cleveland's view that this kind of compromise was wrongheaded. The unyielding opposition to Populist initiatives began to change after Bryan's second defeat, in 1900.[31] And with his third loss, in 1908, reformist Republicans asserted themselves at last.

The initial burst of Progressive constitutionalism during the Taft and Wilson era is best understood as a "second-order" backlash against what was done to stop Bryan in the 1890s.[32] Basically, some of the actions taken in the crisis were now a source of regret and were no longer deemed necessary or appropriate. As I said in chapter 6, there is no such thing as a formal constitutional sunset. Progressive reforms, however, did serve to cut back on the doctrines established when the Populists and those associated with them were scaring many voters. But this backlash to the backlash was quite limited.[33] The doctrines on incorporation and race hardly changed, the liberty of contract was not repudiated, unions were still subject to injunctions, and the Commerce Clause was still read with a restrictive eye. Thus, the essence of the Populist failure remained. The pig just acquired lipstick.[34]

The crucial insight that comes from connecting the Populist backlash to the Progressive movement is that both were unique historical events. In other words, the reason why the Progressives do not look like any other major constitutional mobilization in our history is that they were reacting to the only generational push for reform that failed. One cannot be understood without the other. Calling the Progressive movement a second-order backlash does not deny its influential role in shaping public policy. In the end, however, the legacies of Theodore Roosevelt and Woodrow Wilson pale in comparison to the black hole left behind by Bryan.

Income Taxes and Constitutional Change

The discussion of Progressivism so far has focused on why that movement came about, but it is worth spending some time examining how the change that its supporters sought was implemented. In particular, the debate about how *Pollock* should be overruled raises some fascinating issues.

When the first post-Bryan Congress convened in 1909, the income tax proposal that gained the most traction involved a new statute that would force the Justices to reconsider *Pollock*. A bipartisan group of senators tried to amend a tariff bill to include language nearly identical to that of the 1894 tax statute struck down by the Court.[35] One supporter of the idea explained: "I feel confident that an overwhelming majority of the best legal opinion in this Republic believes that [*Pollock*] was erroneous. With this thought in mind, and remembering that the decision was by a bare majority, and that the decision itself overruled the decisions of a hundred years, I do not think it improper for the American Congress to submit the question to the reconsideration of that great tribunal."[36] The suggestion drew a sharp retort from Senator Albert Beveridge of Indiana, who said that for "sixteen years there has been an increasing distrust of the courts. Nothing could be done that would increase the present suspicion of the courts than to call upon them to reverse themselves."[37] Beveridge did not seem sensitive to the argument that decisions such as *Pollock* were at the heart of the recent distrust, but others shared his apprehension about such a blatant challenge to the Justices.

The Senate bill sparked a deep discussion about judicial review because Congress had never before crafted a statute with the express object of persuading the Court to reverse one of its decisions. Even though the debate focused mostly on the merits of *Pollock*, the institutional question was on everyone's mind. Senator Elihu Root, who had been one of Roosevelt's most trusted cabinet members, said that the legislation would set a bad precedent and harm "the independence, the dignity, the respect, the sacredness of that great tribunal whose function in our system of government has made us unlike any republic that ever existed in the world."[38] Senator Hernando D. Money of Mississippi, on the other hand, ridiculed Root because "I am not one of those who regard the judgment of the Supreme Court as an African regards his deity."[39]

The Senate proposal also led to an extensive colloquy on the rule of law between George Sutherland of Utah, who later became one of the Four Horsemen who fought the New Deal on the Supreme Court, and William Borah of Idaho, who was starting his long career as an advocate for liberal causes. Senator Sutherland posed the following question: "If Congress should now pass that amendment [to the tariff bill], which, as I say, is in identical terms practically with the law already declared to be unconstitutional, what would be the duty of the executive officers of this Government under such circumstances—to follow the decision of the Supreme Court of the United States, which had declared the law unconstitutional, or to follow the law passed by Congress, which has no power to say whether or not in the final analysis the law is constitutional?"[40] Senator Borah replied with a question of his own: "Does the Senator from Utah make no distinction between a law which of itself has been declared unconstitutional and a law similar to it which has been reenacted and which is a reexpression of the legislative power of the Government?"[41] Sutherland answered: "I do not think in principle there is any distinction . . . My judgment is that the executive officers of the Government might well follow the decision of the Supreme Court, because . . . an unconstitutional law is no law. It is so much blank paper."[42] When pressed on whether he meant that citizens should refuse to pay income taxes if the law passed, however, Sutherland refused to take a position.[43]

To avoid these knotty constitutional problems, President Taft sent a special message to Congress. He explained that with respect to the income tax "mature consideration has satisfied me that [a textual] amendment is the only proper course."[44] In Taft's view, "this course is much to be preferred to the one proposed of reenacting a law once judicially declared to be unconstitutional. For the Congress to assume that the court will reverse itself, and to enact legislation on such an assumption, will not strengthen

President William Howard Taft.
Library of Congress.

popular confidence in the stability of judicial construction of the Constitution."[45] Since ratifying the constitutional amendment would take time, the president also proposed that revenue be raised in the interim through new inheritance and corporate taxes, which were more likely to be upheld by the Court.[46]

Critics of *Pollock* were suspicious of this initiative, especially since the compromise received strong support from such conservatives as Senator Aldrich. They thought that proposing a constitutional amendment to allow a federal income tax, and combining it with an alternative tax bill, was little more than a delaying tactic. Borah contended that the "great, controlling, overwhelming proposition, supported by the unquestionable facts surrounding us, is the fact that [the package] is here as a measure to defeat the income tax."[47] The *New York Times* said the corporate and inheritance tax bill was "a brat kidnapped out of the Denver platform of BRYAN, and is now made to serve the political necessities of its foster parents . . . It was accepted by Republican Senators like Mr. ALDRICH, not because they liked it or believed in it—they hate it—but because it was the only means at hand for beating the income tax, which they hated worse."[48] But Taft's proposals moved through Congress with ease, and the Justices unanimously upheld the new corporate tax in 1911.[49]

When the debate on the amendment shifted to the states, the leading critic was none other than Justice Brewer, who was still on the Court. He said that "demagogues and revolutionaries" who wanted to tax the states, "not out of their existence, but out of their vitality" were backing the proposal.[50] Attacking a pending constitutional amendment was an extraordinarily inappropriate action for a sitting Justice, particularly when that amendment was designed to overrule an opinion that he had joined, but it was consistent with Brewer's strong antipathy to anything associated with the Populists. Charles Evans Hughes, who was the governor of New York but who was appointed to the Court in 1910, argued before he put on his judicial robe that the amendment should be rejected because it gave Congress the power to tax state and local bonds. And many of the critics of Bryan's 1894 law, including Joseph H. Choate, came out against the Sixteenth Amendment. Although ratification by the states took three years, supporters did secure enough votes as Taft was leaving office.

Some broader observations are worth making about this substantial constitutional reform, which after all was the first amendment ratified since 1870. First, participants in the congressional debate on the income tax invoked Bryan's name many times to discredit the idea, much as the *New York Times* did. Using the name of someone who held no elective office as an epithet was quite a tribute to Bryan's power as a negative symbol and lends support to the view that his absence was a catalyst for Progressivism. Second, the decision to eliminate *Pollock* rather than Jim Crow or the liberty of contract is emblematic of a certain kind of legal triage (or exercise of judgment) that always follows a generational transition.[51] *Pollock* represented a more dramatic break with prior authority than the other developments in the 1890s; the rest had at least some antecedents. Put another way, in *Pollock* the Justices flouted the normal standards of judicial behavior more flagrantly than in any other contemporary case. Thus, the decision was the most logical (and probably the least popular) one to roll back once a political equilibrium was restored after the "danger" posed by Bryan had passed.

Finally, the discussion about using a statute rather than an Article V amendment to overrule *Pollock* was a preview of the strategy that would be used to great effect during the New Deal. In the 1930s, Republicans did not get the chance to defeat reform by appealing to the Article V amendment process. Congress and the president instead challenged the Court's contrary opinions with laws such as the Fair Labor Standards Act and relied on public opinion to create the switch-in-time that had eluded Bryan.[52] The seeds of the next generational movement were already in the ground, and another turn of the constitutional cycle was at hand.

What Is Constitutional Failure?

An observer who looks at the living reality [of a constitution]
will wonder at the contrast to the paper description. He will see
in the life much which is not in the books; and he will not find
in the rough practice many refinements of the literary theory.
—WALTER BAGEHOT

William Jennings Bryan never held elective office after 1894,
but he exerted more influence over constitutional law than anyone else at the turn of the twentieth century. Bryan's ability to
lose worthy causes with unpersuasive arguments was uncanny.
He failed in 1896 by hitching his star to free silver, in 1900 by
running against imperialism right after the United States won a
popular war, and in 1925 by challenging Social Darwinism with
an attack on Darwin himself, a tactical decision that backfired
in the Scopes Trial and blackened his name forever.[1] But Bryan's unfortunate choice of means should not obscure his role in
bringing about the most profound change in American politics
between Reconstruction and the New Deal.

Even though Bryan's personal journey is compelling, I have
argued in this book that the Populist failure was just one segment

of a constitutional cycle that transcends individuals and is driven by the friction between rival generations. In *Federalist No. 1*, Alexander Hamilton wrote that the debates on the proposed constitution posed the question of "whether societies of men are really capable or not, of establishing good government from reflection and choice, or whether they are forever destined to depend, for their political constitutions, on accident and force."[2] Hamilton knew that most constitutional law is the product of accident and force. It comes from chaotic political competition that upends precedents, revives old opinions, and creates new doctrines whose implications only become clear years later. Passion, not reason, is more often than not the source of America's legal values.

One implication of the constitutional cycle is that judicial interpretation is often an exercise in hiding the differences between generations, not in ascertaining the true meaning of the text or the precedents. The decade of the 1890s is replete with examples of this. When the holding of *Slaughter-House* was rendered obsolete by the backlash against the Populists, the Justices rewrote the decision while claiming that they were honoring it. The liberty of contract was invented to give voice to renewed interest in protecting property rights, and that idea was grafted onto the Fourteenth Amendment because no other portion of the Constitution could bear it. *Marbury* was plucked from relative obscurity to support a broader conception of judicial review than had ever been contemplated before. It was only with the annihilation of voting rights in the South, which was upheld in *Giles*, that the ingenuity of the Court was unable to mask the rupture between past and present. The techniques used in this period can be found at each generational inflection point; scholars should focus attention on how this essential task of melding tradition with democracy must be done. That question is particularly urgent because the Obama generation is now on a collision course with the Court, though that fight is still over the horizon.[3]

Another issue raised by locating the Populists within the constitutional cycle is the impact that this movement had on its generational successor: the New Deal. Franklin D. Roosevelt and William Jennings Bryan look like totally different political leaders, both in their outlook and in their agenda. Nevertheless, we know from the prior turns of the cycle that there must be some connection between the ideology of one cohort and the next because each one reacts to the other.[4] Furthermore, there is a clear structural similarity between the 1890s and the 1930s. In each period, a massive transformation of constitutional doctrine was achieved without an Article V amendment. This point should prompt a deeper inquiry into their relationship.

Although that sort of careful examination cannot be done here, the most interesting thought that emerges is that the New Deal came very close to looking like a rerun of Populism. For instance, a defining feature of the constitutional generation that was in power from 1896 until 1932 was the gold standard, in part because that issue was so central to the McKinley-Bryan campaign. One of President Roosevelt's first acts in 1933 was to repudiate that understanding by taking the United States off the gold standard. When that decision was challenged in the Supreme Court, tensions were extraordinarily high.[5] The president even prepared a radio address in case the Justices ruled against the administration in which he said that he would not comply with the ruling. Luckily, a crisis was averted when the Court rejected the suits by a 5-to-4 vote.[6] If those cases had come out the other way, however, then the issue of monetary policy would have become a crucial one in the 1936 election.

A charismatic politician also presented a Populist alternative to the New Deal: Senator Huey P. Long of Louisiana.[7] Long built a substantial national following with his "Share Our Wealth" movement, which used Bryan's mantra of "Every Man a King, but No Man Wears a Crown."[8] Claiming that the Depression could be ended only through a massive redistribution of income, he fought for a sizeable wealth tax and called for public ownership of large firms. Long was getting ready to run against Roosevelt for the Democratic nomination and, if he lost, to mount a third-party bid in 1936. The president moved to the left to counter this threat, but that confrontation came to a shocking end when Senator Long was assassinated in September 1935. If he had lived, there is every reason to think that the New Deal would have looked more like Bryanism, though how much more is open to debate.

Another line of research that flows from this book is the role that other failures have played in constructing constitutional meaning. One example is the Child Labor Amendment, which Congress passed in the 1920s but which the states never ratified. Though child labor was eventually abolished by other means, the amendment's setback undermined Americans' faith in the Article V process and was exploited by President Roosevelt to justify his Court-packing scheme.[9] The path of the law is littered with similar debacles that merit investigation, even if they lack the glamour of America's constitutional achievements.

Finally, this project raises two questions that have no easy answer. One is whether the 1896 election should be viewed as a failure. I could have called this book *The Amazing William McKinley* and shown how voters mobilized to confront significant constitutional issues in a time of crisis, rendering a powerful verdict in support of McKinley's inspired leadership. After that campaign, I could have argued, the nation recovered from the doom and gloom of the Panic of 1893 and entered a golden era of prosperity and territorial expansion; the Supreme Court codified the electoral mandate in a set of transformative opinions that cast aside tired dogma; and McKinley won an even greater victory in 1900 that ushered in a generation of Republican rule. So why did I decide to present the story the other way around? In part, the answer is normative. It is hard to cheer the loss of voting rights in the South, the imposition of Jim Crow, or some of the other changes of the 1890s, and I am not bound to follow the maxim that winners write history. The events covered by the book were also, I felt, easier to follow when presented from the Populist point of view. That is not the only way to approach the material, of course, and I look forward to other efforts to probe what happened during this era.

The other difficult question is whether Bryan's failure means that heroic constitutional ambitions are too dangerous to pursue. The possibility of a backlash is a powerful reason not to risk controversial reforms; indeed, what unfolded in the 1890s supports that fear. But choosing to suffer silently in the presence of injustice is not without costs. We can see when we look back over the arc of history that the Populists brought new ideas into politics, ideas that fired the imagination of future reformers. William Jennings Bryan and his allies did not prevail in their righteous cause, but their belief in the power of one person to make a difference remains a powerful statement of the American creed for every generation.

Notes

Introduction

1. My distinction between success and failure is artificial in the sense that the opponents of great constitutional landmarks, such as the Anti-Federalists of the 1780s, the secessionists of the 1860s, and the segregationists of the 1960s, do receive attention as the foils of those who achieved success. The point is that scholars do not pay enough attention to unsuccessful popular movements, although there are notable exceptions. See Michael Klarman, *From Jim Crow to Civil Rights* (New York: Oxford University Press, 2004), 385–442 (arguing that the reaction against *Brown v. Board of Education* rallied support for civil rights); Reva B. Siegel, "Constitutional Culture, Social Movement Conflict and Constitutional Change: The Case of the De Facto ERA," *California Law Review* 94 (2006): 1324 (stating that the Equal Rights Amendment "was not ratified, but the amendment's proposal and defeat played a crucial role in enabling and shaping the modern law of sex discrimination. Yet constitutional law lacks tools to explain constitutional change of this kind.").

2. See David R. Mayhew, *Electoral Realignments: A Critique of an American Genre* (New Haven: Yale University Press, 2002), 104–109 (assessing the legislative record). Mayhew is clearly correct about the lack of

congressional action during the McKinley years. In chapter 7, I build on that observation by pointing out that Theodore Roosevelt was far less radical than his current reputation suggests. The flaw in Mayhew's analysis is that he overlooks the constitutional changes that occurred as a result of Bryan's meteoric rise and fall.

3. Ibid. at 104, 112.

4. Stephen Skowronek, *The Politics Presidents Make: Leadership from John Adams to Bill Clinton*, rev. ed. (1993; repr., Cambridge: Harvard University Press, 1997), 48.

5. See Allgeyer v. Louisiana, 165 U.S. 578, 589 (1897) (defining the liberty of contract); see also Lochner v. New York, 198 U.S. 45 (1905) (extending this doctrine and naming an entire era).

6. See O'Neil v. Vermont, 144 U.S. 323, 361–364 (1892) (Field, J., dissenting) (concluding, in a case where the Court declined to reach the merits, that the Cruel and Unusual Punishments Clause applied to the states); ibid. at 370–371 (Harlan, J., dissenting) (same).

7. See Maxwell v. Dow, 176 U.S. 581 (1900) (holding that the rights in the Bill of Rights were not national privileges or immunities); see also Chi., Burlington & Quincy R.R. Co. v. Chicago, 166 U.S. 226 (1897) (holding that the Due Process Clause applied the Takings Clause to the states). Some parts of the Bill of Rights are still not incorporated, although most of them were applied to the states by the 1960s. In the book I use "incorporation" to refer to an extension of the substance of a part of the Bill of Rights to the states. This is a modern term and was not used in the nineteenth-century cases.

8. See United States v. Lopez, 514 U.S. 549, 553 (1995) (stating that until the late nineteenth century "the Court's Commerce Clause decisions dealt rarely with the extent of Congress's power").

9. See In re Debs, 158 U.S. 564 (1895) (upholding the federal government's power to enjoin strikes under the Commerce Clause); United States v. E. C. Knight Co., 156 U.S. 1 (1895) (construing the Sherman Antitrust Act narrowly to avoid constitutional difficulties under the Commerce Clause).

10. See Pollock v. Farmers' Loan & Trust Co., 157 U.S. 429 (1895), modified on rehearing, 158 U.S. 601 (holding that a federal income tax must be apportioned under the Direct Tax Clause). *Pollock* was overruled by the Sixteenth Amendment, which is discussed in chapter 7.

11. See Marbury v. Madison, 5 U.S. (1 Cranch) 137 (1803); Davison M. Douglas, "The Rhetorical Uses of *Marbury v. Madison:* The Emergence of a 'Great Case,'" *Wake Forest Law Review* 38 (2003): 382–397.

12. See Richard H. Pildes, "Keeping Legal History Meaningful," *Constitutional Commentary* 19 (2002): 645 ("Even in the 1890s, half of black men continued to vote in key gubernatorial races in Southern states.").

13. See John D. Hicks, *The Populist Revolt: A History of the Farmers' Alliance and the People's Party* (Lincoln: University of Nebraska Press, 1961), 439–444 (reproducing the Populist Party platform of 1892).

14. "This Week," *The Nation*, November 5, 1896, at 337.

15. See Gerard N. Magliocca, *Andrew Jackson and the Constitution: The Rise and Fall of Generational Regimes* (Lawrence: University Press of Kansas, 2007). The current book draws on the theory of "generational cycles" that I set forth in the Jackson book and explains the concept in greater depth where appropriate.

16. The same generational pattern shapes the evolution of the British Constitution (at least since the Great Reform Act of 1832). The Second Reform Act was enacted in 1867, the "Lords-packing" crisis that gave the House of Commons ultimate authority over lawmaking came in 1911, nationalization and universal health care arrived in 1945, and Thatcherism swept through in the 1980s. See Walter Bagehot, *The English Constitution* (1872; repr., New York: Cosimo Classics, 2007), x–xi (discussing the Reform Act of 1867 and noting that "the 'spirit' of politics is more surely changed by a change of generation in the men than by any other change whatever").

17. Thus, I agree with Michael W. McConnell's view that there was a forgotten constitutional moment when a Jim Crow republic was founded. See Michael W. McConnell, "The Forgotten Constitutional Moment," *Constitutional Commentary* 11 (1994): 115–144. The problem is that his timing is off. McConnell claims that this sea change occurred in 1877, through the compromise that ended the Hayes-Tilden presidential election and led to the withdrawal of Union troops from the South. Ibid. at 122–131. The facts do not support this interpretation, as the analysis in subsequent chapters shows.

18. See Bruce Ackerman, *We the People* (Cambridge: Harvard University Press, 1991), 1:94–103 (arguing that the *Slaughter-House* dissents and *Lochner* represent an internally logical progression from the Fourteenth Amendment); Alexander M. Bickel, "The Original Understanding and

the Segregation Decision," *Harvard Law Review* 69 (1955): 58 (stating the "obvious conclusion" that the Fourteenth Amendment "as originally understood, was meant to apply neither to jury service, nor suffrage, nor anti-miscegenation statutes, nor segregation").

19. See Richard Hofstadter, *The Age of Reform: From Bryan to FDR* (New York: Alfred A. Knopf, 1955), 60–93 (discussing the "folklore of populism").

ONE
Constructing Reconstruction

1. The other natural starting point would be the ratification debates on the Fourteenth Amendment, but I am not interested in whether *Slaughter-House* was consistent with the original understanding or was correct in its reasoning. I am interested only in what *Slaughter-House* said.

2. See Slaughter-House Cases, 83 U.S. (16 Wall.) 36, 57–59, 66 (1873); see also Rogers M. Smith, *Civic Ideals: Conflicting Visions of Citizenship in U.S. History* (New Haven: Yale University Press, 1997), 331 (noting that the butchers could "continue to ply their trade upon payment of a relatively modest, state-regulated fee"); Kevin Christopher Newsom, "Setting Incorporation Straight: A Reinterpretation of the *Slaughter-House Cases*," *Yale Law Journal* 109 (2000): 659–662 (discussing the butchers' argument).

3. See Slaughter-House, 83 U.S. (16 Wall.) at 73–74. For a critical view of this interpretation, see Richard L. Aynes, "Constricting the Law of Freedom: Justice Miller, the Fourteenth Amendment, and the *Slaughter-House Cases*," *Chicago-Kent Law Review* 70 (1994): 644 (stating that the Court's "textual argument, distinguishing between the rights of national citizens and the rights of state citizens, was based upon his deliberate misquotation of Article IV").

4. Slaughter-House, 83 U.S. (16 Wall.) at 76. At this time, civil rights referred to a limited set of topics, so the Court's statement is not as sweeping as it might seem. See Richard A. Primus, *The American Language of Rights* (New York: Cambridge University Press, 1999), 153–160 (discussing the distinction between political, civil, and social rights in the nineteenth century).

5. Slaughter-House, 83 U.S. (16 Wall.) at 78.

6. Ibid. at 89 (Field, J., dissenting); see ibid. at 119 (Bradley, J., dissenting) ("It was not necessary to say in words that the citizens of the United States should have . . . the privilege of buying, selling and enjoying property; the privilege of engaging in any lawful employment for a livelihood.").

7. Ibid. at 96–97 (Field, J., dissenting) (quoting the Civil Rights Act of 1866 and explaining that the "act, it is true, was passed before the fourteenth amendment, but the amendment was adopted, as I have already said, to obviate objections to the act").

8. Ibid. at 97 (Field, J., dissenting); see ibid. at 116 (Bradley, J., dissenting) ("This right to choose one's calling is an essential part of that liberty which it is the object of government to protect; and a calling, when chosen, is a man's property and right."). The rest of Field's opinion discussed common-law authorities condemning monopolies. See ibid. at 102–109 (Field, J., dissenting). If the Privileges or Immunities Clause incorporated the common law, then Field's view of the statute challenged in *Slaughter-House* was probably correct. See ibid. at 105–106 (Field, J., dissenting) ("If the trader in London could plead that he was a free citizen of that city against the enforcement to his injury of monopolies, surely under the fourteenth amendment every citizen of the United States should be able to plead his citizenship of the republic as a protection against any similar invasion of his privileges and immunities.").

9. Ibid. at 110 (Field, J., dissenting).

10. Ibid. at 79.

11. Ibid. at 79–80.

12. See Barron v. Baltimore, 32 U.S. (7 Pet.) 243 (1833).

13. See, e.g., Michael Kent Curtis, *No State Shall Abridge: The Fourteenth Amendment and the Bill of Rights* (Durham, NC: Duke University Press, 1986), 175 ("By its construction of the Fourteenth Amendment [in *Slaughter-House*,] the Court effectively nullified the intent to apply the Bill of Rights to the states."); Bryan H. Wildenthal, "The Lost Compromise: Reassessing the Early Understanding in Court and Congress on Incorporation of the Bill of Rights in the Fourteenth Amendment," *Ohio State Law Journal* 61 (2000): 1063 (stating that "*Slaughter-House* has been conventionally viewed as rejecting incorporation via the Privileges [or] Immunities Clause").

14. See Slaughter-House, 83 U.S. (16 Wall.) at 118–119 (Bradley, J., dissenting) (stating that free speech, free press, jury trial, peaceable assembly, and freedom from unreasonable searches and seizures were secured against state action by the Fourteenth Amendment).

15. See David S. Bogen, "*Slaughter-House* Five: Views of the Case," *Hastings Law Journal* 55 (2003): 343 ("The natural inference is that [the Court] was listing the privileges of national citizenship that existed when the amendment was adopted, not changing their substance."); Newsom, "Setting Incorporation Straight," 678 ("Admittedly, a number of the freedoms [the Court] mentioned—such as the right to access seaports and to use navigable waterways—have little, if anything, to do with the 'Constitution'; they are structural rights.").

16. Slaughter-House, 83 U.S. (16 Wall.) at 79; see also Adamson v. California, 332 U.S. 46, 77 (1947) (Black, J., dissenting) (stating that *Slaughter-House* "enumerated some, but refused to enumerate all of these national rights").

17. See, e.g., Newsom, "Setting Incorporation Straight," 681 ("Having expressly invoked the right of assembly and the privilege of the writ of habeas corpus, it is hard to imagine why Miller would have thought that other textually specified freedoms (including many of those enumerated in the Bill of Rights) should not follow as well."); Wildenthal, "Lost Compromise," 1101–1102 ("Having included habeas corpus and two First Amendment guarantees in such an avowedly nonexhaustive list, what other federal right 'specially designated in the Constitution' could the majority have intended to exclude?"); cf. William Winslow Crosskey, *Politics and the Constitution in the History of the United States* (Chicago: University of Chicago Press, 1953), 2:1128 ("The 'suggestion' of this right was, then, susceptible of being taken as an indication that *all* the rights covered by the first eight amendments had been made good against the states.").

    The Petition Clause reference is ambiguous. It could refer to state action that barred a petition to Congress, or it could mean that the petition right was structural and did not depend on the First Amendment. See United States v. Cruikshank, 92 U.S. (2 Otto.) 542, 552 (1876) ("The very idea of a government, republican in form, implies a right on the part of its citizens to meet peaceably for consultation in respect to public affairs and to petition for a redress of grievances.").

18. See Slaughter-House, 83 U.S. (16 Wall.) at 80; Newsom, "Setting Incorporation Straight," 678 (stating that some of the rights listed by the Court "are uniquely constitutional, protected by the Constitution itself"); cf. Charles R. Pence, "The Construction of the Fourteenth Amendment," *American Law Review* 25 (1891): 548 (stating that *Slaughter-House* "does mention the privilege of the writ of habeas corpus as among the rights of the citizen guaranteed by the Federal constitution and protected from State abridgment by the fourteenth amendment. Now this privilege is granted in the same way and by the same instrument as the immunity from cruel and unusual punishments: The former is conferred by the original constitution and the latter by one of the amendments.").

19. Media and academic responses to the decision did not focus on incorporation either. See Bogen, "*Slaughter-House* Five," 347 ("The incorporation aspect of the *Slaughter-House Cases* was of little interest to contemporaries . . . Academic reaction focused on the majority's rejection of fundamental rights of citizenship, and paid no attention to what that rejection meant for incorporation.").

20. A state case from Utah relied on *Slaughter-House* for its claim that the Fourteenth Amendment has "no application to [criminal] jury trials in state court." State v. Bates, 47 P. 78, 79 (Utah 1896). Another state case from Louisiana could be put in the same category, for that decision cited *Slaughter-House* in order to reject an Establishment Clause claim against a statute that required businesses to close on Sundays. See State ex rel. Walker v. Judge of Sec. A, Crim. Dist. Ct., 39 La. Ann. 132, 136, 1 So. 437, 439 (La. 1887). Before discussing *Slaughter-House*, though, the Court held that the law did not violate the state's Establishment Clause. See ibid. at 136, 1 So. at 440. Thus, the subsequent discussion of the federal claim was on the merits and did not squarely address incorporation.

21. See In re Kemmler, 136 U.S. 436, 448 (1890) (using *Slaughter-House* to make the point about dual citizenship); Cruikshank, 92 U.S. at 549 (citing the case for the idea that "rights of citizenship under one of these governments will be different from those he has under the other").

22. See Maxwell 176 U.S. at 581, 582 (describing the claim); ibid. at 602–605 (rejecting the due process component of this argument).

23. Ibid. at 587.

24. Ibid. at 591; see ibid. at 587–591 (discussing *Slaughter-House*).

25. Slaughter-House, 83 U.S. (16 Wall.) at 72.
26. Ibid. at 70.
27. Ibid. at 71.
28. Ibid. at 81.
29. Munn v. Illinois, 94 U.S. 113, 125 (1877); see ibid. at 134 ("For protection against abuses by legislatures the people must resort to the polls, not to the courts.").
30. Mugler v. Kansas, 123 U.S. 623, 660 (1887).
31. See Stone v. Farmers' Loan & Trust, 116 U.S. 307, 335 (1886) ("General statutes regulating the use of railroads in a state, or fixing maximum rates of charges for transportation, when not forbidden by charter contracts, do not necessarily deprive the corporation owning or operating a railroad within the state of its property without due process of law, within the meaning of the fourteenth amendment of the constitution of the United States, nor take away from the corporation the equal protection of the laws.").
32. See Reagan v. Farmers' Loan & Trust Co., 154 U.S. 362 (1894) (invalidating a state railroad rate scheme as unreasonable under the Equal Protection Clause).
33. Butchers' Union Slaughter-House & Live-Stock Landing Co. v. Crescent City Live-Stock Landing & Slaughter-House Co., 111 U.S. 746, 764 (1884) (Bradley, J., dissenting); see Stone v. Wisconsin, 94 U.S. 181, 186 (1877) (Field, J., dissenting) (stating that *Munn* "destroys all the guaranties of the Constitution and of the common law invoked . . . for the protection of the rights of the railroad companies").
34. See, e.g., In re Jacobs, 98 N.Y. 98, 106–107, 115 (N.Y. 1885) (invalidating a law that barred the manufacture of cigars in tenement houses on due process grounds and stating that liberty "means the right not only of freedom from actual servitude, imprisonment, or restraint, but the right of one to use his faculties in all lawful ways, to live and work where he will, to earn his livelihood in any lawful calling, and to pursue any lawful trade or avocation").
35. See Thomas M. Cooley, *A Treatise on the Constitutional Limitations* (1868; repr., New York: Da Capo Press, 1972), 393 ("If the legislature should undertake to provide that persons following some specified lawful trade or employment should not have capacity to make contracts, or to receive conveyances, or to build such houses as others were allowed to erect, or in any other way to make such use of their property as

was permissible to others, it can scarcely be doubted that the act would transcend the due bounds of legislative power."); William L. Royall, "The Fourteenth Amendment," *Southern Law Review* 4 (1878): 581 (criticizing the Court for rejecting the claims made by the butchers). For an excellent discussion of these issues, see Howard Gilman, *Constitution Besieged: The Rise and Fall of Lochner Era Police Powers Jurisprudence* (Durham, NC: Duke University Press, 1993).

36. See Eilenbacker v. District Court, 134 U.S. 31, 35–39 (1890) (rejecting an argument that the Fourteenth Amendment barred the states from imposing criminal contempt sanctions without a jury); Walker v. Sauvinet, 92 U.S. (2 Otto.) 90, 92 (1876) (holding that the Seventh Amendment "trial by jury in suits at common law pending in the State courts is not . . . a privilege and immunity of national citizenship, which the States are forbidden by the Fourteenth Amendment to abridge"); cf. Missouri v. Lewis, 101 U.S. (11 Otto.) 22, 31 (1880) ("The Fourteenth Amendment does not profess to secure to all persons in the United States the benefit of the same laws and remedies. Great diversities in these respects may exist in two States separated only by an imaginary line. On one side of this line there may be a right of trial by jury, and on the other side no such right. Each state prescribes its own modes of judicial proceedings.").

The statement in the text refers only to cases where the incorporation claim was based on the Fourteenth Amendment and was not procedurally defaulted. See Miller v. Texas, 153 U.S. 535, 538 (1894) ("If the fourteenth amendment limited the power of the states as to such rights, as pertaining to citizens of the United States, we think it was fatal to this claim that it was not set up in the trial court."); Edwards v. Elliott, 88 U.S. (21 Wall.) 532, 557–58 (1874) (dismissing an incorporation claim because "no such error was assigned in the [state court], and . . . the question was not presented to, nor was it decided by, the [state court]").

37. See Downes v. Bidwell, 182 U.S. 244, 282–283 (1901) ("There may be a distinction between certain natural rights enforced in the Constitution by prohibitions against interference with them, and what may be termed artificial or remedial rights that are peculiar to our system of jurisprudence. Of the former class are the rights to one's own religious opinions and to a public expression of them . . . the right to personal liberty and individual property; to freedom of speech, and of the press . . . to immunities from unreasonable searches and seizures, as

well as cruel and unusual punishments, and to other such immunities as are indispensable to free government. Of the latter class are the . . . particular methods of procedure pointed out in the Constitution that are peculiar to Anglo-Saxon jurisprudence, and some of which have already been held by the states to be unnecessary to the proper protection of individuals."); Brown v. New Jersey, 175 U.S. 172, 175 (1899) ("The state is not tied down by any provision of the Federal Constitution to the practice and procedure which existed at common law . . . It may avail itself of the wisdom gathered by the experience of the century to make such changes as may be necessary."); Rowan v. State, 30 Wis. 129, 149–50 (1872) (holding that the Fourteenth Amendment did not require state grand jury indictments since "administration and remedial proceedings must change from time to time with the advancement of legal science and the progress of society").

38. Hurtado v. California, 110 U.S. 516, 530 (1884); see ibid. at 538 ("We are unable to say that the substitution for a presentment or indictment by a grand jury of the proceeding by information after examination and commitment by a magistrate, certifying to the probable guilt of the defendant, with the right on his part to the aid of counsel, and to the cross-examination of the witnesses produced for the prosecution, is not due process of law."). It is fascinating to note—given the current debate about the relevance of international law for interpreting the U.S. Constitution—that the *Hurtado* decision backed the idea. See ibid. at 533 ("There is nothing in *Magna Charta*, rightly construed as a broad charter of public right and law, which ought to exclude the best ideas of all systems and of every age; and as it was the characteristic principle of the common law to draw its inspiration from every fountain of justice, we are not to assume that the sources of its supply have been exhausted.").

39. Ibid. at 532. The text does not distinguish between cases decided under the Due Process Clause (such as *Hurtado*) and those analyzed under the Privileges or Immunities Clause. In my view, the source of the claim did not affect how the Court saw incorporation in this period.

40. Two problematic cases can be distinguished. In *Cruikshank*, the Justices declared that the right of assembly was secured only "against congressional interference. For their protection in its enjoyment, therefore, the people must look to the States." Cruikshank, 92 U.S. at 552. Similarly, they said that the right to bear arms was secured by the Second Amendment, which meant only "that it shall be not be infringed by Congress."

Ibid. at 553. Those critical statements about the incorporation of these substantive rights, however, should be discounted because the case did not involve state action. See ibid. at 554 ("The Fourteenth Amendment prohibits a State from depriving any person of life, liberty, or property, without due process of law, but this adds nothing to the rights of one citizen as against another."); Pence, "Construction of the Fourteenth Amendment," 544 (concluding that *Cruikshank* was not relevant to incorporation due to a lack of state action); Royall, "Fourteenth Amendment," 581–582 (making the same point).

In *Davidson v. New Orleans*, the Court stated that if "private property be taken for public uses without just compensation, it must be remembered that, when the fourteenth amendment was adopted, the provision on that subject, in immediate juxtaposition in the fifth amendment with the one we are construing, was left out." 96 U.S. (6 Otto.) 97, 105 (1878). But this quotation about the incorporation of the Takings Clause was dictum, because the case did not involve a takings claim. The state court opinion in *Davidson*, for example, makes no reference to takings. See In re Commissioners of First Draining Dist., 27 La. Ann. 20 (1875). And when the Justices did extend the Takings Clause to the states, they cited *Davidson* with approval and did not mention its contrary dictum. See Chicago, 166 U.S. at 235.

41. See O'Neil, 144 U.S. at 331 (describing the state court judgment); ibid. at 339 (Field, J., dissenting) (stating that the petitioner was "to be confined at hard labor in the house of correction for the term of 19,914 days,—a period of over 54 years,—a reduction from the term imposed by the justice of the peace of about 25 years").

42. See ibid. at 331–332.

43. See ibid. at 359–360 (Field, J., dissenting) (arguing that when jurisdiction is established, "I think we may look into the whole record" and take up issues that were raised in the state court); ibid. at 370 (Harlan, J., dissenting) (stating that "it is not disputed that [O'Neil] distinctly made this point; and the question was decided against him in the court below. It is true, the assignments of error do not, in terms, cover this point, but it is competent for this court to consider it, because we have jurisdiction."); see also ibid. at 360 (Field, J., dissenting) (stating that "a cruel, as well as an unusual, punishment was inflicted upon the accused"); ibid. at 371 (Harlan, J., dissenting) (reaching the same conclusion).

44. Ibid. at 363 (Field, J., dissenting).

45. Ibid. Justice Field did mention a procedural right—the right against self-incrimination—in his dissent, but his language about the Fourteenth Amendment incorporating "the rights of persons" could be read as creating a distinction between procedural and substantive freedoms, which was necessary in some respect given that the Court had already held that the states were not bound by the civil jury and grand jury requirements of the Bill of Rights.

An earlier Eighth Amendment case rejected incorporation, but that litigation was in the procedural posture of an application for a writ of error, which meant that the Justices took the issue on the merits and assumed *arguendo* that the right applied to the states. See Kemmler, 136 U.S. at 438, 449 (citing an earlier case that was in a similar procedural posture and concluding that the electric chair was not cruel and unusual punishment); see also Ex Parte Spies, 123 U.S. 131, 167–180 (1887) (rejecting incorporation claims related to jury selection on a writ of error application). Another Eighth Amendment opinion, issued a year later, rejected a claim that solitary confinement imposed a week before an execution was cruel and unusual punishment by citing *Kemmler* and strongly suggested that this was also a decision on the merits. See McElvaine v. Brush, 142 U.S. 155, 158–159 (1891).

46. O'Neil, 144 U.S. at 370 (Harlan, J., dissenting); see ibid. at 371 (stating that Justice Brewer concurred "in the main" with Harlan's views). Justice Brewer's role is important because of his change of heart in *Debs*, which is discussed in chapter 4.

47. To some degree, this was the product of luck. Some of the cases presented substantive claims, but these were procedurally defaulted, could be left undecided, or were pleaded incorrectly. See Presser v. Illinois, 116 U.S. 252, 264–265 (1886) (rejecting a Second Amendment claim because it did not refer to the Fourteenth Amendment); Spies, 123 U.S. at 180–181 (concluding that a Fourth Amendment claim was defaulted). Another factor was that grand jury and civil jury rights were usually binary—a defendant either got a jury or did not. Thus, a claim based on the deprivation of one of these rights was more likely to be decided than a claim based on a substantive right, where a court could reject the claim on the merits while assuming *arguendo* that incorporation was valid.

48. See Strauder v. West Virginia, 100 U.S. 303, 310 (1880).

49. See Ex Parte Virginia, 100 U.S. 339, 346–347 (1880).

50. See Yick Wo v. Hopkins, 118 U.S. 356, 373–374 (1886).

51. See Pace v. Alabama, 106 U.S. 583, 585 (1883).

52. See Cruikshank, 92 U.S. (2 Otto.) at 544 (citing the Enforcement Act of 1870); ibid. at 554 (explaining that the Fourteenth Amendment "simply furnishes an additional guaranty against any encroachment by the States upon the fundamental rights which belong to every citizen as a member of society"); ibid. at 556 (stating that in this case "we may suspect that race was the cause of the hostility; but it is not so averred. This is material to a description of the substance of the offence, and cannot be supplied by implication"); Charles Lane, *The Day Freedom Died: The Colfax Massacre, the Supreme Court, and the Betrayal of Reconstruction* (New York: Henry Holt, 2008), 246 (stating that the proof *Cruikshank* sought "was theoretically possible, but very difficult in practice").

53. See Civil Rights Cases, 109 U.S. 3, 9 (1883) (quoting the statutory provision); ibid. at 25 (stating the Court's conclusion). The best discussion of the *Civil Rights Cases* and their relationship to Reconstruction is Richard A. Primus, "The Riddle of Hiram Revels," *Harvard Law Review* 119 (2006): 1716–1730.

54. See Civil Rights Cases, 109 U.S. at 11–12; ibid. at 48 (Harlan, J., dissenting).

55. See Heart of Atlanta Motel v. United States, 379 U.S. 241 (1964).

56. See Paul Finkelman, "Civil Rights in Historical Context: In Defense of *Brown*," *Harvard Law Review* 118 (2005): 985 ("The Northern response to the Court's rejection of racial fairness in the *Civil Rights Cases* was to adopt state laws to accomplish what the Court would not let Congress accomplish.").

57. C. Vann Woodward, *The Strange Career of Jim Crow*, Rev. ed. 1955; repr. (New York: Oxford University Press, 2002), 33.

58. Plessy v. Ferguson, 163 U.S. 537 (1896).

59. Lochner, 198 U.S. at 45.

60. See Robert H. Bork, *The Tempting of America* (New York: Free Press, 1990), 44 (calling *Lochner* "the symbol, indeed the quintessence, of judicial usurpation of power"); see also Lochner, 198 U.S. at 75 (Holmes, J., dissenting) ("The 14th Amendment does not enact Mr. Herbert Spencer's Social Statics.")

61. Most of this criticism is directed at *Slaughter-House* because of the misunderstanding about what that case said. See Charles L. Black, *A New Birth of Freedom* (New Haven: Yale University Press, 1999), 55 (calling

Slaughter-House "probably the worst holding, in its effect on human rights, ever uttered by the Supreme Court"). But the charge could also be leveled at *Maxwell*, in which the Court rejected incorporation even after conceding that members of Congress who ratified the Fourteenth Amendment thought the Bill of Rights was being extended to the states. See Maxwell, 176 U.S. at 601–602 (acknowledging petitioner's citations to the legislative history but stating: "What individual Senators or Representatives may have urged in debate, in regard to the meaning to be given to a proposed constitutional amendment . . . does not furnish a firm ground for its proper construction, nor is it important as explanatory of the grounds upon which the members voted in adopting it").

62. Plessy, 163 U.S. at 551; see Finkelman, "Civil Rights in Historical Context," 979 ("*Plessy* should be understood as an example of judicial villainy; *Brown*, one of judicial heroism.").

63. See Chicago, 162 U.S. at 235–236.

64. Barry Friedman argues that there was a trend in favor of protecting property and contract rights in federal constitutional cases that did not involve the Fourteenth Amendment. See Barry Friedman, *The Will of the People: How Public Opinion Has Influenced the Supreme Court and Shaped the Meaning of the Constitution* (New York: Farrar, Straus and Giroux, 2009), 159–166.

65. See Allgeyer, 165 U.S. at 589.

66. This sudden departure from tradition was on display in the *Pollock* opinions, examined in chapter 4.

67. Chris Guthrie, Jeffrey J. Rachlinski, and Andrew J. Wistrich, "Blinking on the Bench: How Judges Decide Cases," *Cornell Law Review* 93 (2007): 24. For example, it is much easier to connect the dots and see that the September 11 attacks were coming or that we were in a housing bubble in the 2000s after those events happened.

68. This raises another issue. Is my analysis subject to hindsight bias, particularly since I am asserting that the 1890s fits within a deeper cycle of constitutional development? The answer is yes. As a result, after reviewing all of the facts presented in this book, readers must ask themselves whether they think my external political explanation is better than an internal doctrinal one, while recognizing that either explanation is susceptible to hindsight bias. In any case, I have not found many

nineteenth-century writings about doctrine that forecast what came to pass by 1900.

69. Michael Klarman, *From Jim Crow to Civil Rights* (New York: Oxford University Press, 2004), 9–10.

70. Charles Lofgren, *The Plessy Case: A Legal-Historical Interpretation* (New York: Oxford University Press, 1987), 197; see ibid. ("The indifference greeting *Plessy* had a still more fundamental source. Benno Schmidt has labeled the majority opinion 'an untroubled endorsement of racial separation'—and it was.").

71. See Woodward, *Strange Career*, 6 ("What the new status of the Negro would be was not at once apparent, nor were the Southern white people themselves so united on that subject at first as has been generally assumed. The determination of the Negro's place took shape gradually under the influence of economic and political conflicts among divided white people—conflicts that were eventually resolved in part at the expense of the Negro."); Richard H. Pildes, "Keeping Legal History Meaningful," *Constitutional Commentary* 19(2002): 645 ("Contrary to deterministic views of the history of race in late 19th century America, the structure of the 20th century Southern racial order—segregation and the virtual elimination of black citizens from democracy—was not locked into place by some essential, fixed, organic structure of 'the white South' the moment federal troops withdrew.").

72. I discuss this issue more thoroughly in chapters 2 and 3, but one case study on how the Populists prospered in North Carolina is James L. Hunt, *Marion Butler and American Populism* (Chapel Hill: University of North Carolina Press, 2003), 67–139.

73. C. Vann Woodward, "Strange Career Critics: Long May They Persevere," *Journal of American History* 75 (1988): 862.

74. See Finkelman, "Civil Rights in Historical Context," 1002–1003 ("Segregation was not a 'done deal' in the 1890s . . . This is the period that Klarman argues was so racist that the Supreme Court had no choice but to endorse segregation. Yet we can only wonder how much more successful the Populists might have been in their push for racial cooperation if they had had support from the Supreme Court.")

75. There is a circularity problem here, in the sense that someone might think a Populist victory was improbable because racism was endemic. My challenge rests on the fact that the Populists achieved some positive

results with their cooperative agenda and might have gained momentum had the party won at the national level.

76. See Lon L. Fuller, *Legal Fictions* (Stanford, CA: Stanford University Press, 1967), ix ("The fiction finds its most pervasive application in two subjects that seem in other respects at opposite poles from one another: physics and jurisprudence.").

TWO

The Rise of Populism

1. See Edward Irving, *Breakers Ahead! An Answer to the Question Where Are We At?* (Stockton, CA: T. W. Hummel, 1894), 59 ("There is but one party which is ready, willing and eager to tear from off the people the OCTOPUS CLASP of the money power. That party is the PEOPLE'S PARTY."); Andrew Jackson, Veto Message (July 10, 1832), in James D. Richardson, ed., *A Compilation of the Messages and Papers of the Presidents, 1789–1897* (Washington, DC: Government Printing Office, 1899), 2:590 (vetoing the Bank of the United States because "many of our rich men have not been content with equal protection and equal benefits, but have besought to make them richer by act of Congress").

2. Compare Joel H. Silbey, ed., *The American Party Battle: Election Campaign Pamphlets, 1828–1876* (Cambridge: Harvard University Press, 1999), 1:16 (quoting a Jacksonian mantra that "the only use of government is . . . to [keep] off evil. We do not want its assistance in seeking after good"), with William A. Peffer, *Populism, Its Rise and Fall* (1899; repr., Lawrence: University Press of Kansas, 1992), 175 ("Populists believe in the exercise of national authority in any and every case where the general welfare will be promoted thereby."); see also Roscoe C. Martin, *The People's Party in Texas: A Study in Third Party Politics* (Austin: University of Texas, 1933), 96 ("The People's Party went out to the limit of its means after the colored vote; it recognized the importance of that vote; and it worked long and diligently in its effort to convert it to Populism.").

3. See Bruce Ackerman, *We The People* (Cambridge: Harvard University Press, 1991), 1:84 (describing Populism as a failed constitutional moment).

4. See generally Nassim Nicholas Taleb, *The Black Swan: The Impact of the Highly Improbable* (New York: Random House, 2007) (discussing these

sorts of extraordinary events and criticizing how most people assess the risk that they pose). There are constitutional black swans: the 1935 assassination of Senator Huey P. Long ("The Kingfish") is one example. See Gerard N. Magliocca, "Huey P. Long and the Guarantee Clause," *Tulane Law Review* 83 (2008): 36–43 (discussing the impact of Long's death on the New Deal). What I am saying is that popular movements are not random or unpredictable.

5. See Letter from Thomas Jefferson to James Madison (September 6, 1789), in *The Papers of Thomas Jefferson*, ed. Julian P. Boyd (Princeton, NJ: Princeton University Press, 1958), 15:396 (making this argument because "the earth belongs to the living").

6. The only exception to this pattern was the rapid turnaround between Lyndon B. Johnson's landslide in 1964, which validated the cause of civil rights, and Ronald Reagan's conservative sweep in 1980, which established a conservative majority until 2008. I do not have a satisfying explanation for this deviation from the norm, but my suspicion is that the realignment of a one-party region (the South) following the Voting Rights Act of 1965 was the principal factor.

7. Many constitutional changes result from mass mobilizations that focus on a particular issue (for example, women's suffrage) or are produced by gradual adaptation in accord with common-law methods. Consequently, I am not saying that the constitutional generations described in the text are the only popular movements that matter or are the only engine of legal reform.

8. For a superb analysis of how cyclical behavior drives the financial system, see Charles P. Kindleberger et al., *Manias, Panics, and Crashes: A History of Financial Crises* (Hoboken, NJ: John Wiley and Sons, 2005).

9. See Thomas Kuhn, *The Structure of Scientific Revolutions* (Chicago: University of Chicago Press, 1996).

10. See Steven D. Levitt and Stephen J. Dubner, *Freakonomics: A Rogue Economist Explores the Hidden Side of Everything* (New York: William Morrow, 2005), 184–188 (discussing the rotation in baby names); Kal Raustiala and Christopher Sprigman, "The Piracy Paradox: Innovation and Intellectual Property in Fashion Design," *Virginia Law Review* 92 (2006): 1721–1722 (explaining the fashion cycle).

11. See generally Norman Ryder, *The Cohort Approach: Essays in the Measurement of Temporal Variations in Demographic Behavior* (New York: Arno Press, 1980) (discussing this concept); see also Norval D. Glenn,

"Distinguishing Age, Period, and Cohort Effects," in Jeylan T. Mortimer and Michael J. Shanahan, eds., *Handbook of the Life Course* (New York: Kluwer Academic/Plenum, 2003), 465 (discussing "cohort effects"); and David E. Bernstein and Ilya Somin, "Judicial Power and Civil Rights Reconsidered," *Yale Law Journal* 114 (2004): 615 ("Political scientists and sociologists have for a long time realized that people's views on controversial political and ideological issues are often critically dependent on generation-specific formative experiences."). This does not mean that all people who are the same age think alike. Nor am I saying that people never change their minds about politics. The point is that age is a reference point that has predictive power.

12.   See Richard H. Thaler and Cass R. Sunstein, *Nudge: Improving Decisions about Health, Wealth, and Happiness* (New Haven: Yale University Press, 2007), 25.

13.   The rise of the abolitionists is discussed in my book about Jacksonian Democracy; see Gerard N. Magliocca, *Andrew Jackson and the Constitution: The Rise and Fall of Generational Regimes* (Lawrence: University Press of Kansas, 2007), 88–90, in which I show how the generational cycle unfolded from 1819 until 1870.

14.   Walter Bagehot, *The English Constitution*, (1872; repr., New York: Cosimo Classics, 2007), xii.

15.   See H. W. Brands, *The Reckless Decade: America in the 1890s* (New York: St. Martin's, 1995), 199; see also John D. Hicks, *The Populist Revolt: A History of the Farmers' Alliance and the People's Party* (Lincoln: University of Nebraska Press, 1961), 301–302.

16.   See Lawrence Goodwyn, *The Populist Moment: A Short History of the Agrarian Revolt in America* (New York: Oxford University Press, 1978), 16–17.

17.   See Brands, *Reckless Decade*, 22–27; see generally Frederick Jackson Turner, *The Frontier in American History* (New York: H. Holt, 1920).

18.   See C. Vann Woodward, *Tom Watson: Agrarian Rebel* (New York: Macmillan, 1938), 129–131; see also James L. Hunt, *Marion Butler and American Populism*, (Chapel Hill: University of North Carolina Press, 2003), 23 (stating that merchants commonly charged a 50 percent interest rate in rural areas).

19.   See Richard Hofstadter, *The Age of Reform: From Bryan to FDR* (New York: Alfred A. Knopf, 1955), 58 (stating that farmers faced a "high cost

of credit," "discriminatory railroad rates," and "unreasonable elevator and storage charges").

20. See Irving, *Breakers Ahead!* 33 ("We have over us the money king, the iron king, the coal king, the cattle king, the pork king, the wheat king, the corn king, the lumber king, the railroad magnate, the telegraph monopolist, and the coffin despot.").

21. Thomas E. Watson, *The People's Party Campaign Book, 1892* (1892; repr., New York, Arno Press, 1975), 206–207.

22. See Hicks, *Populist Revolt*, 27–28, 96–97; Stanley L. Jones, *The Presidential Election of 1896* (Madison: University of Wisconsin Press, 1964), 74.

23. See Goodwyn, *Populist Moment*, 27; see also Brands, *Reckless Decade*, 184 ("While farmers watched the corporations with which they did business get larger and more consolidated, they increasingly felt the need to consolidate in self-defense.").

24. See Hicks, *Populist Revolt*, 103; Woodward, *Tom Watson*, 136.

25. Brands, *Reckless Decade*, 184 (quoting the *Chicago Western Rural*).

26. See Hicks, *Populist Revolt*, 427–430 (quoting the Saint Louis Demands); see also Hunt, *Marion Butler*, 30 (calling this "first platform [of the Farmers' Alliance] expressing a unitary set of national political demands").

27. The best presentation of the Populist passion for silver is William H. Harvey, *Coin's Financial School* (1894; repr., Cambridge: Harvard University Press, 1963), a fictional account of a teenager who debates the issue with the financial titans of Chicago. The book, which was, after all, about a dry topic, became a sensation. See Louis W. Koenig, *Bryan: A Political Biography of William Jennings Bryan* (New York: Putnam, 1971), 158 ("Seldom, if ever, has a publication educated so vast a public on a serious political issue."). As I explain in chapter 5, however, not all Populists believed that the silver issue was the most important one.

28. Michael Kazin, *A Godly Hero: The Life of William Jennings Bryan* (New York: Alfred A. Knopf, 2006), 61.

29. Hicks, *Populist Revolt*, 90.

30. Ibid. at 427–428 (quoting the Saint Louis Demands).

31. See ibid. at 428 ("We demand that the means of communication and transportation shall be owned by and operated in the interest of the people as is the United States postal system.").

32. See Edward Bellamy, *Looking Backward, 2000–1887* (1888; repr., New York: Signet Classic, 2000); see also Owen M. Fiss, *Troubled Beginnings*

of the Modern State, 1888–1910, vol. 8 of *History of the Supreme Court of the United States* (New York: Macmillan, 1993), 38 (stating that *Looking Backward* sold more copies than any other nineteenth-century book except for *Ben-Hur* and *Uncle Tom's Cabin*). Bellamy may not have had AIG in mind when he was describing the wonders of nationalization.

33. Woodward, *Tom Watson*, 260 (quoting Tom Watson's article on "the railroad question").

34. See "The Omaha Platform," in Hicks, *Populist Revolt*, 443 (stating the official positions of the Populist Party during the 1892 presidential campaign); see also T. C. Jory, *What Is Populism? An Exposition of the Principles of the Omaha Platform Adopted by the People's Party in National Convention Assembled* (Salem, OR: R. E. Moores, 1895), 9 ("Every citizen of the United States who wishes to do so shall have an opportunity to go to work directly for his government.").

35. Martin Ridge, *Ignatius Donnelly: The Portrait of a Politician* (Chicago: University of Chicago Press, 1962), 324.

36. "Omaha Platform," 440.

37. See ibid. at 444.

38. See Hicks, *Populist Revolt*, 432, 434–435 (collecting various resolutions of the Farmers' Alliance prior to the Omaha Platform).

39. "Omaha Platform," 441.

40. Ibid. at 444; see ibid. at 443 (discussing alien ownership).

41. See Hofstadter, *Age of Reform*, 82.

42. William H. Carwardine, *The Pullman Strike* (1894; repr., Chicago: Charles H. Kerr, 1973), 121; see Dred Scott v. Sandford, 60 U.S. (19 How.) 393, 407 (1857) (stating that the Framers believed that African Americans "had no rights which the white man was bound to respect"); see also James B. Weaver, *A Call to Action: An Interpretation of the Great Uprising, Its Sources and Causes* (Des Moines: Iowa Printing, 1892), 133 ("We distinctly remember that the same Court and Dred Scott once differed in their conceptions of human rights under our Constitution. But Dred Scott's views are now generally accepted. It is probable that the controversy between the farmers and the Court will end in the same way.").

43. The best biography of General Weaver is Robert B. Mitchell, *Skirmisher: The Life, Times, and Political Career of James B. Weaver* (Roseville, MN: Edinborough Press, 2008).

44. See Julliard v. Greenman, 110 U.S. at 421, 450 (1884) (holding that the creation of legal tender was a political question committed to the sole discretion of Congress); Springer v. United States, 102 U.S. 586, 602 (1881) (upholding a federal income tax).

45. See Hunt, *Marion Butler*, 42; see also Weaver, *Call to Action*, 5 ("The sovereign right to regulate commerce among our magnificent union of States, and to control the instruments of commerce . . . have been leased to associated speculators.").

46. See James B. Weaver, "The Threefold Contention of Industry," in Vernon Rosco Carstensen, ed., *Farmer Discontent, 1865–1900* (New York: John Wiley and Sons, 1974), 82; see also Pauline Maier, *American Scripture: Making the Declaration of Independence* (New York: Random House, 1997), 202–206 (recounting Lincoln's use of the Declaration of Independence in his arguments against slavery).

47. Weaver, "Threefold Contention," 82; see Jory, *What Is Populism?* 15 (stating that a "man's right to life involves his right to occupy a place to live on. Some place to live on is a necessary condition to life itself.").

48. Weaver, "Threefold Contention," 84. For a thoughtful discussion on Populist constitutional ideas, see William E. Forbath, "Caste, Class, and Equal Citizenship," *Michigan Law Review* 98 (1999): 43–49.

49. See Bowman v. Chi. & Nw. Ry. Co. 125 U.S. 465, 498–500 (1888) (striking down state laws barring the importation of liquor without a license); Wabash, St. Louis & Pac. Ry. Co. v. Illinois, 118 U.S. 557, 577 (1886) (holding that the regulation of interstate railroad rates could only "be done by the Congress of the United States under the commerce clause of the Constitution"); Weaver, *Call to Action*, 111–125 (arguing that these cases were inconsistent with the precedents governing the police power of the states when Congress did not act). Weaver was also worried that the Court could overturn its decisions against the application of the Fourteenth Amendment to state regulation, as it "was the purpose in certain circles to overthrow . . . the Grange decisions of 1876." Weaver, *Call to Action*, 84–85.

50. Weaver, "Threefold Contention," 84. Weaver quotes the Commerce Clause in full in this particular article.

51. Ibid.; see Weaver, *Call to Action*, 410 ("The power which the people originally possessed to regulate commerce among the States for themselves was by the adoption of the Constitution, solemnly transferred to

Congress and . . . the Congress can not escape the responsibility if it would.").

52. Hunt, *Marion Butler*, 42 (internal quotation marks omitted).

53. Weaver, "Threefold Contention," 85–86; see Weaver, *Call to Action*, 265–266 (comparing Congress's actions to granting letters of marque to privateers).

54. Weaver, *Call to Action*, 436.

55. Gibbons v. Ogden, 22 U.S. (9 Wheat.) 1 (1824).

56. See Civil Rights Cases, 109 U.S. 3 (1883); Trade-Mark Cases, 100 U.S. 82 (1879); Knox v. Lee, 79 U.S. (12 Wall.) 457 (1871); Dred Scott, 60 U.S. (19 How.) at 393; M'Culloch v. Maryland, 17 U.S. (4 Wheat.) 316 (1819). In the *Trade-Mark Cases*, counsel did suggest that the Commerce Clause could sustain a federal law regulating marks, but the Court declined to address the issue because Congress did not consider that option. See 100 U.S. at 94–98. The Court said in the *Civil Rights Cases* that the issue of whether Congress could prohibit private racial discrimination under the commerce power was not raised (see 109 U.S. at 19), but the argument was in one of the briefs. I thank Richard Primus for pointing this out to me.

57. See Sherman Antitrust Act, ch. 647, 26 Stat. 209 (1890); Interstate Commerce Act, ch. 104, 24 Stat. 379 (1887); see also Lopez, 514 U.S. at 549, 554 ("These laws ushered in a new era of federal regulation under the commerce power.").

58. See William Letwin, *Law and Economic Policy in America: The Evolution of the Sherman Antitrust Act* (New York: Random House, 1965), 88 (describing Sherman's view that "the only constitutional provision enabling Congress to legislate against trusts was the power to levy taxes").

59. See 21 Cong. Rec. 2562, 2562 (1890) (statement of Sen. Sherman); Letwin, *Law and Economic Policy*, 89; Robert P. Faulkner, "The Foundations of Noerr-Pennington and the Burden of Proving Sham Petitioning: The Historical-Constitutional Argument in Favor of a 'Clear and Convincing' Standard," *University of San Francisco Law Review* 28 (1994): 697–699 (stating that Sherman was well aware of Farmers' Alliance lobbying efforts on behalf of the Interstate Commerce Act and antitrust legislation).

60. See Gibbons, 22 U.S. (9 Wheat.) at 189 ("Commerce, undoubtedly, is traffic, but it is something more: it is intercourse.")

61. See Gerard N. Magliocca, "A New Approach to Congressional Power: Revisiting the *Legal Tender Cases*," *Georgetown Law Journal* 95 (2006): 124–149 (discussing the star-crossed history of *M'Culloch*).

62. See Gerald H. Gaither, *Blacks and the Populist Movement: Ballots and Bigotry in the New South* (Tuscaloosa: University of Alabama Press, 2003), 97–113 (exploring racism within the Southern Populist movement).

63. Ibid. at 82; see William Warren Rogers Sr., *The One-Gallused Rebellion: Agrarianism in Alabama, 1865–1896* (Tuscaloosa: University of Alabama Press, 2001), 333 ("To ascribe to the Populists a sustained and righteous desire to correct the wrongs done to the Negroes in Alabama is to overstate the case. Yet the Populists promoted the cause of the Negroes, admitted them to their councils, and advocated their political and economic advancement.").

64. See Richard H. Pildes, "Democracy, Anti-Democracy, and the Canon," *Constitutional Commentary* 17 (2000): 300 ("Black (male) political participation remained extraordinarily high long after federal military forces were withdrawn from the South in 1877.").

65. See Joseph Columbus Manning, *Fadeout of Populism* (New York: T. A. Hebbons, 1928), 35 ("The People's Party . . . did bring to the South its first real democracy and the only democracy the South has ever known."); see also Alex Mathews Arnett, *The Populist Movement in Georgia: A View of the "Agrarian Crusade" in the Light of Solid-South Politics* (New York: Columbia University, 1922), 133 (quoting Donnelly's view that the Populists intended "to wipe out the color line" in politics). The text is referring to Populist Party members, not just any self-styled "populist" politician.

66. C. Vann Woodward, *The Strange Career of Jim Crow*, rev. ed. (1955; repr., New York: Oxford University Press, 2002), 64; see Martin, *People's Party in Texas*, 93 ("The first convention of the party recognized him by appointing as members of its State Executive Committee two negroes for the State at large, and subsequent conventions likewise flattered the black in ways designed to win his support." (internal citation omitted)).

67. "Georgia Populists Platform," *People's Party Paper*, September 11, 1896, at 8; see Woodward, *Tom Watson*, 239–240 (describing one such incident and stating that "the spectacle of white farmers riding all night to save a Negro from lynchers was rather rare in Georgia" until the Populists

came along). Even though this quotation comes from the 1896 platform, it reflects a position that was taken much earlier.

68.   Rogers, *One-Gallused Rebellion*, 313; see Woodward, *Strange Career*, 64
("Populist sheriffs saw to it that Negroes appeared for jury duty; and
Populist editors sought out achievements of Negroes to praise in their
columns.").

69.   Woodward, *Tom Watson*, 220 (quoting Watson's 1892 article entitled
"The Negro Question in the South"); see Arnett, *Populist Movement in
Georgia*, 151 (expressing the view of a racist historian of the Dunning
School who said that "Watson had an insolent negro friend campaign-
ing in his behalf? What might such an alliance bring forth!" (footnote
omitted)).

70.   B. T. Harvey, "Some Reasons Why the Negroes of Georgia Should
Support the People's Party State Platform and Nominees," *People's
Party Paper* September 11, 1896, at 8.

71.   Ibid.

72.   See Gaither, *Blacks and the Populist Movement*, 77; Mitchell, *Skirmisher*,
169–171; see also Woodward, *Tom Watson*, 220 (quoting Watson's view
that "Bryan had no everlasting and overshadowing Negro Question to
hamper and handicap his progress: I HAD").

73.   Like many liberals in the twentieth century, Bryan complained about
southern resistance to activist government. See Kazin, *Godly Hero*, 147
(telling southern leaders privately that they were "opposed to government ownership because you are afraid your Jim Crow laws against the
negroes will be abolished by the general government. As if your personal objections to riding with negroes should interfere with a great
national reform."). Bryan's own views on race, however, were rather
conventional for a white man. See ibid. at 278–279 (quoting Bryan's
draft memoir in which he stated his pride in being "a member of the
greatest of all the races, the Caucasian race").

74.   See James L. Sundquist, *Dynamics of the Party System: Alignment and
Realignment of Political Parties in the United States* (Washington, DC:
Brookings Institute, 1983), 136–137. Weaver carried Colorado, Idaho,
Kansas, Nevada, and North Dakota. See Hicks, *Populist Revolt*, 263
(displaying a map with the distribution of the Populist vote).

75.   See Hicks, *Populist Revolt*, 267; see also Jones, *Presidential Election of 1896*,
77 (stating that "the first Populist successes in the West in 1891 and 1892
were spectacular for a political movement so recently established").

76. Irving, *Breakers Ahead*, 37.
77. Ibid. at 15.

THREE

Resistance North and South

1. The term "mutual transformation" comes from war theory. See Carl von Clausewitz, *On War* (1832; repr., Princeton, NJ: Princeton University Press, 1984), 75–77; see also Garry Wills, *Certain Trumpets: The Call of Leaders* (New York: Simon and Schuster, 1994), 86 (calling mutual transformation the idea that "each side is increasingly enraged by the other's efforts to meet violence with greater violence").

2. See Herbert Croly, *Marcus Alonzo Hanna: His Life and Work* (New York: Macmillan, 1912), 210 ("The business depression, coincident with Mr. Cleveland's second administration, stirred the American people more deeply and had graver political consequences than had any previous economic famine."); see also George A. Akerlof and Robert J. Shiller, *Animal Spirits: How Human Psychology Drives the Economy, and Why It Matters for Global Capitalism* (Princeton, NJ: Princeton University Press, 2009), 59–64 (providing an excellent overview of the panic).

3. My working definition of a backlash is "counterforces unleashed by threatening changes to the status quo." See Robert Post and Reva Siegel, "*Roe* Rage: Democratic Constitutionalism and Backlash," *Harvard Civil Rights–Civil Liberties Law Review* 42 (2007): 389.

4. The vanquished of one era could, it is true, be turned back into heroes by a subsequent generation. This is basically what happened with John Marshall and his opinions in *Worcester v. Georgia* and *M'Culloch v. Maryland*, which were deemed failures by Jacksonian Democrats and models by Reconstruction Republicans.

5. Thomas Hart Benton, *An Examination of the Dred Scott Case* (New York: D. Appleton, 1857), 123. Benton was President Jackson's principal ally in the Senate during the 1830s.

6. See Reva B. Siegel, "Constitutional Culture, Social Movement Conflict and Constitutional Change: The Case of the De Facto ERA," *California Law Review* 94 (2006): 1364 ("As a countermovement begins persuasively to rebut new constitutional claims, a movement for social change has incentives to qualify its claims so that those claims are likely to be understood as a reasonable account of the tradition to those whom the

movement must persuade. The countermovement is of course subject to the same constraints.").

7. See ibid. at 1331 ("During the ERA campaign, hope of the amendment's ratification led many in the women's movement to define sex discrimination narrowly in matters concerning reproduction and sexuality in order to respond to concerns raised by the traditional-family-values movement. At the same time, fear of the amendment's ratification led many in the traditional-family-values movement to defend gender roles in egalitarian terms in order to address concerns raised by the women's movement.").

8. Ibid. at 1330.

9. Ibid.

10. Indeed, one could say that polarization is what distinguishes constitutional politics from ordinary politics. Siegel's framework builds on basic insights about how bills get passed by seeking a compromise, which can apply to constitutional and non-constitutional issues. But constitutional politics with a capital *C* breaks with these rules, as is explained in the text.

11. Clausewitz, *On War*, 69; see Richard A. Posner, *An Affair of State* (Cambridge: Harvard University Press, 1999), 248–258 (relying on Clausewitz's analysis to explain the Clinton impeachment saga).

12. This quotation and the two preceding ones are from Clausewitz, *On War*, 76; see ibid. (explaining that once enemy resistance is assessed "you can adjust your own efforts accordingly . . . But the enemy will do the same; competition will again result and, in pure theory, it must again force you both to extremes"). There is also a rational component to escalation. As each side invests more effort in its campaign to overcome the other, they might feel that a higher payoff is necessary to justify the costs.

13. Ibid. at 118; see ibid. at 117 (discussing the concept of friction in war and noting that soldiers "tend to exaggerate the bad news").

14. For a sense of how conservatives were terrified by the Populists, see Barry Friedman, *The Will of the People: How Public Opinion Has Influenced the Supreme Court and Shaped the Meaning of the Constitution* (New York: Farrar, Straus and Giroux, 2009), 172–173.

15. The *Pollock* case discussed in chapter 4 is a key example from the Populist era, but other excellent ones are *Worcester v. Georgia* (against the Jacksonian generation) and *Dred Scott* (against the Republican genera-

tion). See Gerard N. Magliocca, *Andrew Jackson and the Constitution: The Rise and Fall of Generational Regimes* (Lawrence: University Press of Kansas, 2007), 42–50, 100–109.

16. See Post and Siegel, *"Roe* Rage," 376–377 ("Contemporary scholarly debate does not sufficiently appreciate the ways that citizen engagement in constitutional conflict may contribute to social cohesion in a normatively heterogeneous polity.")

17. Allan Nevins, *Grover Cleveland: A Study in Courage* (New York: Dodd, Mead, 1932), 649.

18. See Grover Cleveland, Inaugural Address (March 4, 1893), in James D. Richardson ed., *A Compilation of the Messages and Papers of the Presidents 1789–1897* (Washington, DC: Government Printing Office, 1899) 9:390 ("While people should patriotically and cheerfully support their Government its functions do not include the support of the people.").

19. See Louis W. Koenig, *Bryan: A Political Biography of William Jennings Bryan* (New York: Putnam, 1971), 132–133; "History of the Income-Tax Law," *New York Times*, April 9, 1895, at 3 ("The authorship of the income tax has been variously credited to Mr. McMillin of Tennessee and Mr. Byran [*sic*] of Nebraska.").

20. The act required the Treasury to purchase silver with notes that could be redeemed in gold or silver. See H. W. Brands, *The Reckless Decade: America in the 1890s* (New York: St. Martin's, 1995), 83; Jean Strouse, *Morgan: American Financier* (New York: Random House, 1999), 305.

21. See James L. Hunt, *Marion Butler and American Populism* (Chapel Hill: University of North Carolina Press, 2003), 61; see also Grover Cleveland, Special Session Message (August 8, 1893), in Richardson, *Messages and Papers*, 402–403 (outlining the president's opposition to the Silver Purchase Act of 1890).

22. See Strouse, *Morgan*, 341–349; see also Grover Cleveland, Annual Message (December 2, 1895), in Richardson, *Messages and Papers*, 644 ("With a reserve perilously low and a refusal of Congressional aid, everything indicated that the end of gold payments by the Government was imminent . . . An agreement was therefore made with a number of financiers and bankers.").

23. Hunt, *Marion Butler*, 68 (internal quotation marks omitted).

24. C. Vann Woodward, *Tom Watson: Agrarian Rebel* (New York: Macmillan, 1938), 252–253; cf. Strouse, *Morgan*, 350 ("No President for two

decades forgot the intensity of public outrage at Washington's deal with Wall Street.").

25. Woodward, *Tom Watson*, 253.

26. Brands, *Reckless Decade*, 171–173.

27. Strouse, *Morgan*, 336.

28. In re Debs, 158 U.S. 564 (1895) (upholding an injunction issued against the leaders of the Pullman Strike).

29. The background of the strike is summarized in Brands, *Reckless Decade*, 147–150; and David Ray Papke, *The Pullman Case* (Lawrence: University Press of Kansas, 1999), 11–35.

30. Papke, *Pullman Case*, 19; see Brands, *Reckless Decade*, 148–149.

31. See Brands, *Reckless Decade*, 150; see also Owen M. Fiss, *Troubled Beginnings of the Modern State, 1888–1910*, vol. 8 of *History of the Supreme Court of the United States* (New York: Macmillan, 1993), 73 ("The Chicago disturbance started as an ordinary strike but quickly took on extraordinary dimensions. It created a mass disorder, paralyzing the national rail and postal systems and threatening the very idea of an economic union.").

32. Papke, *Pullman Case*, 35 (internal quotation marks omitted).

33. Woodward, *Tom Watson*, 261 (quoting Attorney General Olney).

34. See Fiss, *Troubled Beginnings*, 65; see also Brands, *Reckless Decade*, 153 ("Among business circles Altgeld possessed a reputation as a flaming radical . . . [who] consistently took the side of labor in industrial quarrels.").

35. I do not deny that there was a plausible case for federal action during the Pullman Strike, although a lot of work was required to develop a rationale. But see David Gray Adler, "The Steel Seizure Case and Inherent Presidential Power," *Constitutional Commentary* 19 (2002): 184–185 (calling Cleveland's justification "altogether unpersuasive").

36. See Debs, 158 U.S. at 568–572; see also Brands, *Reckless Decade*, 151 (observing that railroad officials forcibly halted mail trains).

37. Proclamation No. 11 (July 8, 1894), 28 Stat. 1249 (1894), in Richardson, *Messages and Papers*, 499; see Brands, *Reckless Decade*, 152 (laying out the timeline).

38. All of the quotations in this paragraph and the next from the Altgeld-Cleveland correspondence come from W. F. Burns, *The Pullman Boycott* (Saint Paul: McGill Printing Co., 1894), 63–65.

39. Brands, *Reckless Decade*, 153 (internal quotation marks omitted); see Matthew Josephson, *The Politicos, 1865–1896* (New York: Harcourt, Brace, 1938), 587 ("The respectable press of the country is a unit in applauding and sustaining the President." (quoting *The Nation* of July 12, 1894)).

40. Burns, *Pullman Boycott*, 45; see Papke, *Pullman Case*, 38.

41. See *Republican Campaign Text-Book* (Washington, DC: Hartman and Cadick, 1896), 138; see also Delmore Elwell, *A Wall Street View of the Campaign Issues of 1896* (New York: Published by the author, 1896), 4 (discussing the "railroad strike riots of 1894" and stating that "there are still a few blue-coated veterans of the Civil War who will . . . register a prayer for a revival of the spirit of 1860").

42. Burns, *Pullman Boycott*, 113 (quoting a letter sent by local activists to the national chair of the Populist Party).

43. *Republican Campaign Text-Book*, 138 (quoting the 1896 Democratic Party Platform).

44. U.S. Const. art. IV, § 4; see William J. Bryan, *The First Battle: A Story of the Campaign of 1896* (Chicago: W. B. Conkey, 1896), 410 (quoting his letter accepting the Democratic nomination); see also *Campaign Text-Book of the National Democratic Party* (Chicago: National Democratic Committee, 1896), 1.93 (quoting the attorney general's response to Bryan). The "National Democratic Party" was the faction that supported Cleveland and walked out of the Democratic convention in 1896. They were referred to as "Gold Democrats," and that is how I will describe them.

45. Bryan, *First Battle*, 411; see *Campaign Text-Book of the National Democratic [Gold] Party*, 1.93.

46. *Republican Campaign Text-Book*, 138; see "The Nation's Honor Must Be Preserved," *Harper's Weekly*, September 26, 1896, at 938 ("In 1861, some of the States undertook to enforce the doctrine that the Federal government had not the power to prevent them from leaving the Union . . . To-day Mr. Bryan is asserting that the Federal government cannot enforce its laws or protect its property against the violence of mobs except by the consent of the State.").

47. This quotation and the next two in the text come from the *Campaign Text-Book of the National Democratic [Gold] Party*, 1.91, 1.93. Just as there was a contradiction in the Populists' support for nationalization and

argument for states' rights when it came to labor injunctions, so, too, the establishment was talking at cross-purposes when it argued for a strong federal role in labor disputes but a hands-off approach elsewhere.

48. See U.S. Const. art. I, § 10, cl. 5 ("No State shall . . . make any Thing but gold and silver Coin a Tender in Payment of Debts."); ibid. art. I, § 10, cl. 8 (stating that no state can enact any "Law impairing the Obligation of Contracts"); see also Barron v. Baltimore, 32 U.S. (7 Pet.) 243 (1833) (holding that the original Constitution did not apply the Bill of Rights to the states).

49. Presser, 116 U.S. at 252, 268. *Presser* involved a claim by a workers' militia that an Illinois statute prohibiting private armed groups from marching without a license violated the First and Second Amendments. See ibid. at 264–265 (rejecting Presser's Second Amendment argument because Presser did not cite the Fourteenth); ibid. at 267 (stating that the First Amendment "petition and assembly" right was a national privilege or immunity but concluding that the militia in *Presser* was not engaged in petitioning activity).

50. See William Warren Rogers Sr., *The One-Gallused Rebellion: Agrarianism in Alabama, 1865–1896* (Tuscaloosa: University of Alabama Press, 2001), 332 ("The Democrats adroitly used the Negro issue to brand Populism as a threat to Southern institutions and to indict its leaders as either traitors or misguided idealists."); see also C. Vann Woodward, *The Strange Career of Jim Crow*, rev. ed. (1955; repr., New York: Oxford University Press, 2002), 79 ("Alarmed by the success that the Populists were enjoying with their appeal to the Negro voter, the conservatives themselves raised the cry of 'Negro domination' and white supremacy, and enlisted the Negrophobe elements.").

51. See Gerald H. Gaither, *Blacks and the Populist Movement: Ballots and Bigotry in the New South* (Tuscaloosa: University of Alabama Press, 2003), 56 (stating that the result of the Force Bill "was a reassessment of individual regional loyalties" and white solidarity).

52. See Howard N. Rabinowitz, *Race Relations in the Urban South, 1865–1890* (Athens: University of Georgia Press, 1996), 333–339. Howard Rabinowitz was C. Vann Woodward's main jousting partner and brought forth crucial evidence about the informal segregation and exclusion that existed prior to the 1890s. I do not dispute that evidence. My claim is that de jure Jim Crow, which Rabinowitz concedes emerged only in the 1890s, was partly caused by the Populist backlash.

53. See Charles Lofgren, *The Plessy Case: A Legal-Historical Interpretation* (New York: Oxford University Press, 1987), 24 (noting that "the agrarian movement in several states probably contributed support to separate car measures"). Indeed, Martin Luther King Jr. took this position in his speech at Selma in 1965. See Woodward, *Strange Career*, 231–232 (quoting King's view that "racial segregation as a way of life did not come about as a natural result of the hatred between the races immediately after the Civil War . . . As the noted historian, C. Vann Woodward, in his book, *The Strange Career of Jim Crow*, clearly points out, the segregation of the races was really a political stratagem employed by the emerging Bourbon interests in the South to keep the Southern masses divided and Southern labor the cheapest in the land.").

54. Michael Klarman points out that the railroads opposed this regulation because providing separate cars was expensive. See Michael Klarman, *From Jim Crow to Civil Rights* (New York: Oxford University Press, 2004), 18.

55. Lofgren, *Plessy Case*, 22. Florida passed a statute in 1887 that applied only to first-class cars, whereas a pre-1891 Texas law only authorized (as opposed to mandating) the segregation of railroads. See ibid.

56. See Klarman, *From Jim Crow to Civil Rights*, 48.

57. Lofgren, *Plessy Case*, 22 (pointing out that South Carolina, North Carolina, Virginia, Maryland, and Oklahoma passed railroad segregation after 1898).

58. James Andrew Mead, "The Populist Party in Florida" (master's thesis, Florida Atlantic University, 1971), 53; see ibid. at 79 (quoting the Democratic view that "the real issue of the campaign was not the money question at all, but the race question . . . If the Populists or Republicans won the October election, the supremacy of the white race in Florida would be threatened").

59. Rogers, *One-Gallused Rebellion*, 312; see ibid. at 214 (stating that Democrats could not "afford to endorse that 'nigger rights' section" in the Alliance platform of 1892).

60. Hunt, *Marion Butler*, 148.

61. Woodward, *Tom Watson*, 370; see Hunt, *Marion Butler*, 152 (quoting a speech by Butler in which he attacked the Democrats by asking: "My fellow citizens, what is their creed and doctrine today? On the first page there is but one thing. What is it? 'Nigger'"); see also John D. Hicks, *The Populist Revolt: A History of the Farmers' Alliance and the People's Party*

(Lincoln: University of Nebraska Press, 1961), 348 (quoting a declaration by the Democratic Party convention in Mississippi, which stated that they afford the "only security for the maintenance of white supremacy in the state, and that all political movements which tend to divide or weaken our party are in direct conflict with the true interests of the state . . . We therefore deplore the movement now afoot for the organization of a third party, to be known as the People's party.").

62. See Woodward, *Tom Watson*, 236–241 (describing the climate of fear that pervaded the 1892 campaign in Georgia); see also Joel Williamson, *The Crucible of Race: Black-White Relations in the American South since Emancipation* (New York: Oxford University Press, 1984), 117 ("Beginning in the year 1889, in the South and in the nation at large, the lynching of Negroes increased markedly and within a few years reached its height.").

63. Williamson, *Crucible of Race*, 117.

64. See Alex Mathews Arnett, *The Populist Movement in Georgia: A View of the "Agrarian Crusade" in the Light of Solid-South Politics* (New York: Columbia University, 1922), 153 ("Intimidation, bribery, ballot-box stuffing, and manipulation of the count, while deplored, were thought to be lesser evils than the loss of political control by the 'respectable' elements and the jeopardizing of the social order."); see also Rogers, *One-Gallused Rebellion*, 282 (stating that the "election methods were so illegal that several Democratic papers protested"); Burton D. Wechsler, "Black and White Disenfranchisement: Populism, Race, and Class," *American University Law Review* 52 (2002): 29 ("The Populist agenda was too dangerous, Populist appeal too popular, Populist growth too alarming, and the enormity of the black belt fraud too embarrassing for the Bourbons to shoulder.").

65. Arnett, *Populist Movement*, 168–170 (quoting Letter from William J. Northen, Governor of Georgia, to Grover Cleveland, President of the United States (September 15, 1893)).

66. Ibid. at 169. The next quotation in the text is also on this page.

67. Papke, *Pullman Case*, 32.

68. Woodward, *Tom Watson*, 262; see Martin Ridge, *Ignatius Donnelly: The Portrait of a Politician* (Chicago: University of Chicago Press, 1962), 334.

69. James L. Sundquist, *Dynamics of the Party System: Alignment and Realignment of Political Parties in the United States* (Washington, DC: Brookings Institute, 1983), 149.

70. See Richard Hofstadter, *The Age of Reform: From Bryan to FDR* (New York: Alfred A. Knopf, 1955), 100; see also Sundquist, *Dynamics of the Party System*, 149 (stating that the party's vote went from one million to one and a half million).

71. See Sundquist, *Dynamics of the Party System*, 149 (describing the huge Republican victory in 1894 with a gain of 117 House seats).

72. Frank Basil Tracy, "Rise and Doom of the Populist Party," in Vernon Rosco Carstensen, ed., *Farmer Discontent, 1865–1900* (New York: John Wiley and Sons, 1974).

FOUR

The Supreme Court Intervenes

1. Robert H. Jackson, *The Struggle for Judicial Supremacy* (New York: Alfred A. Knopf, 1941), 315. For a compelling account of the generational clash during the 1930s, which touches on Jackson's role in the Court-packing crisis, see Jeff Shesol, *Supreme Power: Franklin Roosevelt vs. The Supreme Court* (New York: W.W. Norton, 2010).

2. See Matthew Josephson, *The Politicos, 1865–1896* (New York: Harcourt, Brace, 1938), 605 ("By a series of fateful decisions in 1895, with which it intervened boldly in the controversies of the age, the Supreme Court . . . assumed the commanding role in our Government. It was a kind of legal 'revolution' or coup d'état.").

3. See Northern Securities Co. v. United States, 193 U.S. 197, 400–401 (1904) (Holmes, J., dissenting) ("Great cases, like hard cases, make bad law. For great cases are called great, not by reason of their real importance in shaping the law of the future, but because of some accident of immediate overwhelming interest which appeals to the feelings and distorts the judgment. These immediate interests exercise a kind of hydraulic pressure which makes what previously was clear seem doubtful, and before which even well settled principles of law will bend.").

4. The first person to observe that judicial behavior varies with the strength of the coalition in power was Woodrow Wilson, in his *Congressional Government: A Study in American Politics* (1885; repr., New York: Meridian Books, 1956), 45 ("It has been only during comparatively short periods of transition, when public opinion was passing over from one political creed to another, that the decisions of the federal

judiciary have been distinctly opposed to the principles of the ruling political party.").

5. See Gerard N. Magliocca, *Andrew Jackson and the Constitution: The Rise and Fall of Generational Regimes* (Lawrence: University Press of Kansas, 2007), 42–50, 100–109 (discussing *Worcester* and *Dred Scott*); see also United States v. Callender, 25 F. Cas. 239 (C.C.D. Va. 1800) (No. 14,709) (Chase, J.) (displaying the same traits at the turn between the Federalist and the Jeffersonian generations).

6. Reagan, 154 U.S. at 362.

7. Ibid. at 412–413.

8. Ibid. at 399; see ibid. at 410 ("The equal protection of the laws—the spirit of common justice—forbids that one class should, by law, be compelled to suffer loss that others may make gain.").

9. See ibid. at 409–410; see also ibid. at 410 ("Is it any less a departure from the obligations of justice to seek to take, not the title, but the use, for the public benefit, at less than its market value?")

10. E. C. Knight, 156 U.S. at 1.

11. See William H. Carwardine, *The Pullman Strike* (1894; repr., Chicago: Charles H. Kerr, 1973), 93; see also E. C. Knight, 156 U.S. at 19 (Harlan, J., dissenting) (implying that sugar was "essential to the comfort of every household in the land").

12. E. C. Knight, 156 U.S. at 12.

13. Ibid.

14. Ibid. at 13.

15. *Gibbons* was cited once for a general (and boilerplate) definition of commerce. See E. C. Knight, 156 U.S. at 12. The other reference came when *Gibbons* was distinguished because in that case "the state laws, which were held inoperative, were instances of direct interference with, or regulations of, interstate or international commerce." See ibid. at 15–16.

16. Ibid. at 14 (quoting Kidd v. Pearson, 128 U.S. 1, 20 (1888)).

17. Ibid. at 15.

18. Ibid.

19. Ibid. at 19–21, 36, 45 (Harlan, J., dissenting); see also Owen M. Fiss, *Troubled Beginnings of the Modern State 1888–1910*, vol. 8 of *History of the Supreme Court of the United States* (New York: Macmillan, 1993), 115 (stating that Harlan focused on the impact of the regulated activity

on commerce rather than on the activities that could be regulated). It would be misleading to say that Harlan's reading of *Gibbons* means that the case was important all along and that everyone else (the Populists, President Cleveland, and the other eight Justices) who failed to cite it were missing the boat. A better description would be that Justice Harlan was being creative (just as Joseph H. Choate would be with respect to *Marbury*) and developed a valuable interpretive resource for succeeding generations.

20. E. C. Knight, 156 U.S. at 35–36 (Harlan, J., dissenting).
21. Ibid. at 37.
22. Ibid. at 24.
23. Ibid. at 44.
24. Pollock 157 U.S. 429, modified on rehearing, 158 U.S. 601. For the sake of clarity in the citations, I will designate the first part of the case as *Pollock I* and the part after the rehearing petition as *Pollock II*.
25. See "Senator Hill Is Elated," *New York Times*, April 9, 1895, at 3 (quoting the senator's view that that the income tax was "pressed upon Congress by a lot of Populists, Socialists, cranks, and disturbers . . . It was class legislation of the worst kind"); cf. Delmore Elwell, *A Wall Street View of the Campaign Issues of 1896* (New York: Published by the author, 1896), 3–4 (stating that an income tax would "change the character of the people, to reorganize them also, changing honest citizens into perjured liars and to set loose on the community a body of sneaking detectives").
26. Springer, 102 U.S. at 586, 602.
27. See Scholey v. Rew, 90 U.S. (23 Wall.) 331, 351 (1874) (rejecting a challenge to inheritance taxes); Veazie Bank v. Fenno, 75 U.S. (8 Wall.) 533, 549 (1869) (rejecting a challenge to taxes on state bank notes); Pacific Ins. Co. v. Soule, 74 U.S. (7 Wall.) 433, 446 (1868) (upholding a tax on insurance premiums); Hylton v. United States, 3 U.S. (3 Dall.) 171 (1796) (upholding an excise tax on carriages).
28. U.S. Const. art I, § 2, cl. 3; see ibid. art I, § 9, cl. 4 ("No capitation, or other direct, Tax shall be laid, unless in Proportion to the Census or Enumeration herein before directed to be taken.")
29. Hylton, 3 U.S. (3 Dall.) at 177 (opinion of Patterson, J.).
30. See Pollock II, 158 U.S. at 684 (Harlan, J., dissenting) (arguing that the Court "interprets constitutional provisions, originally designed to

protect the slave property against oppressive taxation, as to give privileges and immunities never contemplated by the founders of the government"); ibid. at 687 (Brown, J., dissenting) (explaining that the Direct Tax Clauses were "adopted for a special and temporary purpose, that passed away with the existence of slavery").

31. Josephson, *Politicos*, 610; see Pollock I, 157 U.S. at 532 (argument of Mr. Choate, Attorney for Appellants) (stating that the income tax was "communistic in its purposes and tendencies, and is defended here upon principles as communistic, socialistic . . . as ever have been addressed to any political assembly in the world").

32. Josephson, *Politicos*, 610; see Pollock I, 157 U.S. at 533 (argument of Mr. Choate, Attorney for Appellants) (stating that if the Court took no action "this communistic march goes on").

33. Pollock I, 157 U.S. at 531–532 (argument of Mr. Carter, Attorney for Appellee).

34. Ibid. at 553 (argument of Mr. Choate, Attorney for Appellants).

35. Pollock II, 158 U.S. at 674 (Harlan, J., dissenting).

36. See Charles Evans Hughes, *The Supreme Court of the United States, Its Foundation, Methods, and Achievements: An Interpretation* (Garden City, NY: Garden City Publishing Co., 1936), 52–55. Hughes was right to compare *Pollock* with *Dred Scott* because both were preemptive opinions that came at inflection points between constitutional generations.

37. See Pollock I, 157 U.S. at 609–612 (White, J., dissenting) (making this point); see also ibid. at 653 (Harlan, J., dissenting) ("Giving due effect to the statutory provision that 'no suit for the purpose of restraining the assessment or collection of any tax shall be maintained in any court,' the decree below dismissing the bill should be affirmed." (citation omitted)).

38. Ibid. at 554. The Court also suggested that this was a suit to prevent the misappropriation of corporate funds rather than a claim to restrain tax collection. See ibid. That argument is unpersuasive. Since the point of limiting the judiciary's equitable power was to prevent tax collection from being hindered, allowing an exception for corporate shareholders would seriously disrupt the federal scheme.

39. See Pollock II, 158 U.S. at 618 ("Our previous decision was confined to the consideration of the validity of the tax on the income from real estate, and on the income from municipal bonds."); Fiss, *Troubled Beginnings*, 76 (discussing Justice Jackson's illness).

40. Pollock II, 158 U.S. at 618 ("We are now permitted to broaden the field of inquiry . . . [to] a tax upon a person's entire income.").

41. Pollock I, 157 U.S. at 554 (quoting *Marbury*).

42. See Davison M. Douglas, "The Rhetorical Uses of *Marbury v. Madison:* The Emergence of a 'Great Case," *Wake Forest Law Review* 38 (2003): 376–377; see also ibid. at 382–386 (showing that treatises either ignored or dismissed *Marbury* before the 1890s).

43. See ibid. at 387–397.

44. See ibid. at 395 ("During the ninety-two years between *Marbury* and *Pollock*, the Court had never once seen it necessary when declaring a congressional statute unconstitutional to defend its power to exercise judicial review by reference to the authority of an earlier decision.").

45. See, e.g., Walter Bagehot, *The English Constitution* (1872; repr., New York: Cosimo Classics, 2007), 291 (stating that "anomalies, in a hundred instances, mark out the old boundaries of a constitutional struggle. The casual line was traced according to the strength of deceased combatants; succeeding generations fought elsewhere; and the hesitating line of a half-drawn battle was left to stand for a perpetual limit").

46. This quotation is attributed to many people. Mark Twain, Otto von Bismarck, and Thomas Reed are three other possible sources.

47. Pollock I, 157 U.S. at 583; see ibid. at 559–569 (discussing the Framers and the economists); see also Pollock II, 158 U.S. at 629–632 (discussing the English authorities).

48. Pollock I, 157 U.S. at 583.

49. The Court conceded that when a delegate at the Constitutional Convention asked for "the precise meaning of direct taxation. No one answered." Ibid. at 563; see ibid. at 614 (White, J., dissenting) ("It will, in my opinion, serve no useful purpose . . . to seek to ascertain the meaning of the word 'direct' in the Constitution by resorting to the theoretical opinions on taxation found in the writings of some economists."); see also *Pollock II*, 158 U.S. at 684 (Harlan, J., dissenting) (attacking the majority for interpreting "constitutional provisions, originally designed to protect the slave property against oppressive taxation, as to give privileges and immunities never contemplated by the founders of the government").

50. Pollock II, 158 U.S at 641 (Harlan, J., dissenting).

51. The view that land taxes were direct was established in the Court's first case on the Direct Tax Clauses. See Hylton, 3 U.S. (3 Dall.) at 174

(opinion of Chase, J.) ("The direct taxes contemplated by the Constitution, are only two, to wit, a capitation . . . and a tax on land."). The rationale for calling land taxes direct was similar to the one for slaves: it alleviated sectional strife by barring small states from using their power in the Senate to tax large states.

52. See Springer, 102 U.S. at 602 (upholding an income tax and stating "that direct taxes, within the meaning of the Constitution, are only capitation taxes, as expressed in that instrument, and taxes on real estate"); Scholey, 90 U.S. (23 Wall.) at 347–348 (stating that a direct tax "does not include the tax on income").

53. Pollock II, 158 U.S. at 626. Compare Pollock I, 157 U.S. at 571–572 (arguing that in *Hylton* the Court "distinctly avoided expressing an opinion upon that question or laying down a comprehensive definition, but confined [each] opinion to the case before the court"), and Pollock II, 158 U.S. 626–627 (same), with Pollock I, 157 U.S. at 616–620 (White, J., dissenting) (explaining that the reasoning in *Hylton* was contrary to the majority's analysis), and ibid. at 619 (stating that in "the decision in that case the legislative department of the government has accepted the opinions . . . as conclusive in regard to the meaning of the word 'direct'").

54. Pollock I, 157 U.S. at 573 (internal quotation marks omitted).

55. Ibid. at 574.

56. In a related case, the Court upheld the use of paper money during the Civil War as a wartime exigency, which suggests that the omission of that explanation in *Springer* is telling. See Knox, 79 U.S. (12 Wall.) at 457, 550–551 (ruling that Congress has implied power in wartime that it would not have in peacetime).

57. Pollock I, 157 U.S. at 608 (White, J., dissenting); see ibid. at 652 (White, J., dissenting) ("Let it be felt that on great constitutional questions this court is to depart from the settled conclusions of its predecessors, and to determine them all according to the mere opinion of those who temporarily fill its bench, and our constitution will . . . be bereft of value.").

58. Francis R. Jones, *"Pollock v. Farmers' Loan and Trust Company," Harvard Law Review* 9 (1895): 198.

59. Pollock II, 158 U.S. at 662–663 (Harlan, J., dissenting).

60. Ibid. at 706 (Jackson, J., dissenting).

61. Edward S. Corwin, "The *Dred Scott* Decision in the Light of Contemporary Legal Doctrines," *American History Review* 17 (1911): 66.

62. Pollock II, 158 U.S. at 596 (Field, J., concurring); see David G. Farrelly, "Justice Harlan's Dissent in the *Pollock* Case," *Southern California Law Review* 24 (1951): 179 (stating Justice Harlan's view that "Field acted often like a mad man during the whole of this contest about the income tax").

63. Pollock II, 158 U.S. at 695 (Brown, J., dissenting); see ibid. (stating that this could be "the first step toward the submergence of the liberties of the people in a sordid despotism of wealth"); see also Farrelly, "Justice Harlan's Dissent," 177 (describing the Justice's oral dissent).

64. "Income Tax Law Dead," *New York Times*, May 21, 1895, at 1.

65. "Tax Is Knocked Out," *Chicago Tribune*, May 21, 1895, at 3.

66. "The Income-Tax Decision," *The Nation*, May 23, 1895, at 394.

67. Alan Furman Westin, "The Supreme Court, the Populist Movement and the Campaign of 1896," *Journal of Politics* 15 (1953): 22.

68. See Debs, 158 U.S. at 573 (describing the habeas petition); see also H. W. Brands, *The Reckless Decade: America in the 1890s* (New York: St. Martin's, 1995), 159; David Ray Papke, *The Pullman Case* (Lawrence: University Press of Kansas, 1999), 71.

69. Brands, *Reckless Decade*, 158; see Papke, *Pullman Case*, 63 (describing their argument that upholding the injunction would "turn over the workingmen of this country, bound hand and foot, to the mercy of corporate rapacity and greed" (internal quotation marks omitted)).

70. Papke, *Pullman Case*, 63. An interesting aside is that Justice Harlan sensed this danger and, in a private letter to the district judge presiding over *Debs*, urged him to set aside the contempt order on remand. See L. H. LaRue, "Constitutional Law and Constitutional History," *Buffalo Law Review* 36 (1987): 390 ("If Debs and his companions remain in jail during the summer, are they not likely to be regarded as martyrs by a large number of people? . . . I take it that you could, if you saw proper, set aside the order fining and imprisoning and discharge the parties in contempt." (quoting letter from Justice Harlan to Judge W. A. Woods (May 28, 1895)).

71. See Debs, 158 U.S. at 600. The Court's approach was also troubling given that the only issue presented in *Debs* was whether there was jurisdiction to hear the habeas petition. See Fiss, *Troubled Beginnings*,

61 ("According to the standard rule, the Court was not to determine whether the injunction that Debs had disobeyed was appropriately issued . . . The only issue open for review was whether the circuit court had jurisdiction.").

72.   Debs, 158 U.S. at 577; see Fiss, *Troubled Beginnings*, 61–62 (remarking that the case "raised profound questions about the constitutional system and called for answers that were couched in the highest terms of generality").

73.   Debs, 158 U.S. at 581.

74.   Ibid. at 582.

75.   Papke, *Pullman Case*, 64 (internal quotation marks omitted); see Josephson, *Politicos*, 606 (explaining that an injunction "was a formidable legal weapon, making possible imprisonment for contempt of court without a hearing, and without trial by jury, of those who organized labor action").

76.   Debs, 158 U.S. at 581–582.

77.   Ibid. at 582.

78.   Ibid. at 592.

79.   Ibid. at 598–599.

80.   "The Debs Insurrection Unlawful," *Chicago Tribune*, May 28, 1895, at 6.

81.   Norman Pollock, ed., *The Populist Mind* (Indianapolis: Bobbs-Merrill, 1967), 8 (quoting a speech from a Kansas Populist leader who attacked the circuit court decision in *Debs* for holding that "you have no right to convince a man to your opinion. You have no right to ask a man to quit work today, no matter what the cause. This is the position that some of the United States Courts have taken today. This is whither we are driven."). A similar point was made about the attacks on Coxey's Army. Ibid. at 345 (quoting a Nebraska newspaper editorial arguing that the attacks were an infringement on the Petition Clause).

82.   Budd v. New York, 143 U.S. 517, 551 (1892) (Brewer, J., dissenting).

83.   Fiss, *Troubled Beginnings*, 56.

84.   Ibid. at 56–57.

85.   Brands, *Reckless Decade*, 159.

86.   Ibid.

87.   Ibid. at 160.

88.   "The Week," *The Nation*, May 30, 1895, at 413.

89.   See Josephson, *Politicos*, 611 (quoting the *New York Tribune*'s view that "the fury of ignorant class hatred . . . has dashed itself in vain against

the Constitution of the United States"); "Debs Insurrection Unlawful," at 6 (noting that *Debs* "is the second defeat the Populists and demagogues have met with at the hands of the Supreme Court this year").

90. Indeed, Plessy's lawyers wanted the case heard after the election, although their rationale was unrelated to Bryan or the Populists. See Charles A. Lofgren, *The Plessy Case: A Legal-Historical Interpretation* (New York: Oxford University Press, 1987), 150 (quoting one of the attorneys who hoped that Thomas Reed, McKinley's rival for the Republican nomination, would be elected and take a stronger stand on civil rights).

91. Plessy, 163 U.S. at 537, 560 (Harlan, J., dissenting). Harlan's dissents in *Plessy* and *Pollock* were linked by his argument that the Court read Reconstruction too narrowly. See Bruce Ackerman, "Taxation and the Constitution," *Columbia Law Review* 99 (1999): 30 ("Of course, this interpretive turn is expressed differently in the two cases—in *Plessy*, by upholding racial subordination; in *Pollock*, by expanding the constitutional bargain with slavery.").

92. In *Plessy* the Court glossed over this point by stating that the Louisiana legislature was "at liberty to act with reference to the established usages, customs, and traditions of the people" when it enacted Jim Crow. Plessy, 163 U.S. at 550–551. This statement is wonderfully ambiguous. If it refers to legal customs, then the quotation is misleading because no tradition of segregation existed in the South prior to the 1890s. If, on the other hand, the Court meant to invoke norms that did not rise to the level of statutory law, then the statement is valid. Someone reading the opinion, however, could come away from it thinking that the Justices were just ratifying a well-established legal regime instead of sanctioning a recent innovation.

93. "Equality, but Not Socialism," *New Orleans Daily Picayune*, May 19, 1896, at 4.

94. Brown v. Board of Education, 347 U.S. 483 (1954).

95. Brief for Appellants in Nos. 1, 2, and 4 and for Respondents in No. 10 on Reargument at 61–62, Brown v. Board of Education, 347 U.S. 483 (1954). The briefs in *Brown* are now approaching canonical status. See Parents Involved in Cmty. Schs. v. Seattle Sch. Dist., 551 U.S. 701, 747 (2007) (opinion of Roberts, C.J.) (quoting the NAACP brief in *Brown* as support for a race-blind principle).

96. T. C. Jory, *What Is Populism? An Exposition of the Principles of the Omaha Platform Adopted by the People's Party in National Convention Assembled* (Salem, OR: R. E. Moores, 1895), 13.

FIVE

The Election of 1896

1. For a useful summary of this discussion about fusion, see Lawrence Goodwyn, *The Populist Moment: A Short History of the Agrarian Revolt in America* (New York: Oxford University Press, 1978), 230–249. Every third party eventually faces this problem.

2. H. W. Brands, *The Reckless Decade: America in the 1890s* (New York: St. Martin's, 1995), 270 (quoting Tom Watson); see Alex Mathews Arnett, *The Populist Movement in Georgia: A View of the "Agrarian Crusade" in the Light of Solid-South Politics* (New York: Columbia University, 1922), 190 (quoting Watson's editorial against fusion).

3. John D. Hicks, *The Populist Revolt: A History of the Farmers' Alliance and the People's Party* (Lincoln: University of Nebraska Press, 1961), 327.

4. See ibid. at 344 (quoting Weaver's view that: "I shall favor going before the people in 1896 with the money question alone, unencumbered with any other contention whatsoever").

5. Another consideration is that there were pro-silver Republicans in the West (in areas where there were mines). Although these delegates, led by Senator Henry Teller of Colorado, did walk out after McKinley was nominated, their support for Bryan proved underwhelming. See Hicks, *Populist Revolt*, 351–354 (assessing the Teller boomlet); see also James L. Hunt, *Marion Butler and American Populism* (Chapel Hill: University of North Carolina Press, 2003), 97–98 (discussing Butler's efforts to court Senator Teller).

6. See Brands, *Reckless Decade*, 282–283 ("It was hard for city-dwelling factory workers to get excited . . . Higher prices for wheat and cotton meant little to them except higher prices for bread and clothes.").

7. See ibid. at 270; see also James L. Sundquist, *Dynamics of the Party System: Alignment and Realignment of Political Parties in the United States* (Washington, DC: Brookings Institute, 1983), 153 (quoting Lloyd's view that "if we fuse, we are sunk. If we don't fuse, all the silver men we have will leave us for the more powerful Democrats").

8. Marion Butler supported independence but agreed with the move to postpone the Populist convention because he thought that the Democrats would choose a gold nominee. See Hunt, *Marion Butler*, 95. Given the efforts of the fusionists to shift the Populist convention to a later date, it would appear that Butler was naive.

9. See Michael Kazin, *A Godly Hero: The Life of William Jennings Bryan* (New York: Alfred A. Knopf, 2006), 46–48, 52–53. The rest of the detail in this paragraph also comes from portions of the Kazin biography.

10. Goodwyn, *Populist Moment*, 247.

11. Governor Altgeld probably would have been nominated (at a convention in his state) had he been a native-born citizen. See Brands, *Reckless Decade*, 258; see also U.S. Const., art. II., § 4 ("No Person except a natural born Citizen . . . shall be eligible to the Office of President.").

12. At this time, the Democratic national convention required a nominee to win two-thirds of the delegate votes. Thus, a determined minority like the gold faction could block a candidate.

13. James Lowry Whittle, *Grover Cleveland* (London: Bliss, Sands, 1896), 239.

14. Brands, *Reckless Decade*, 257.

15. Ibid. at 258.

16. Kazin, *Godly Hero*, 55.

17. Ibid. at 61.

18. Brands, *Reckless Decade*, 260.

19. Kazin, *Godly Hero*, 61.

20. Louis W. Koenig, *Bryan: A Political Biography of William Jennings Bryan* (New York: Putnam, 1971), 188.

21. Bruce Ackerman, "Taxation and the Constitution," *Columbia Law Review* 99 (1999): 31 n.119.

22. See Hicks, *Populist Revolt*, 354.

23. The Gold Democrat ticket ended up with only about 1 percent of the popular vote.

24. W. D. Bynum, "Address Before the National Democratic Party," in *Campaign Text-Book of the National Democratic Party* (Chicago: National Democratic Committee, 1896), 4.

25. Ibid. at 6.

26. Hicks, *Populist Revolt*, 357–358.

27. See Hunt, *Marion Butler*, 103.

28. This confusing (but juicy) exercise in chicanery is discussed in Goodwyn, *Populist Moment*, 259–263.
29. See Hunt, *Marion Butler*, 116.
30. See Robert W. Cherny, *A Righteous Cause: The Life of William Jennings Bryan* (Norman: University of Oklahoma Press, 1994), 70; see also Sundquist, *Dynamics of the Party System*, 162 ("The massive swing to the Republicans in the North was predominately urban."). Bryan did carry Denver, but it was not a big city then.
31. See Brands, *Reckless Decade*, 281.
32. For a fine discussion of this aspect of the presidency, see generally Jeffrey K. Tulis, *The Rhetorical Presidency* (Princeton, NJ: Princeton University Press, 1987). Bryan was not the first candidate to campaign personally, as I erroneously stated in an earlier article of mine. See Kazin, *Godly Hero*, 67 (noting that Horace Greeley and James G. Blaine had done so). He does appear to be the first to ever speak on his own behalf (albeit indirectly) at a convention. Franklin D. Roosevelt was the first major party candidate to give an acceptance speech in the modern sense.
33. See "Bryan the Demagogue," *New York Times*, July 11, 1896, at 3; "The One Issue," *New York Times*, July 11, 1896, at 4; "W. J. Bryan, Populist," *New York Times*, July 26, 1896, at 1.
34. James A. Barnes, "Myths of the Bryan Campaign," in George F. Whicher, ed., *William Jennings Bryan and the Campaign of 1896* (Boston: D. C. Heath, 1953), 73 (internal quotation marks omitted); see "The Week," *The Nation*, July 16, 1896, at 39 (describing the "overpowering necessity of keeping the Tillmans, Blands, Bryans, Altgelds, and the indescribables who believe them to be statesmen, out").
35. Douglas Dutro Woodard, "The Presidential Election of 1896" (master's thesis, Georgetown University, 1949), 352 (quoting a letter from John Hay to Henry Adams dated August 4, 1896); see *Republican Campaign Text-Book* (Washington, DC: Hartman and Caddick, 1896), 4 ("Its majority is simply a howling mob of Populists, free-silverites and Anarchists, dominated by Altgeld.").
36. See Brands, *Reckless Decade*, 269.
37. The best recent account of McKinley, which may fairly be called revisionist, is Kevin Phillips, *William McKinley* (New York: Henry Holt, 2003).

38. See Kazin, *Godly Hero*, 66 (quoting McKinley's view that "I might just as well put up a trapeze on my front lawn and compete with some professional athlete as go out speaking against Bryan").

39. See Brands, *Reckless Decade*, 274; see also Edmund Morris, *The Rise of Theodore Roosevelt* (New York: Modern Library, 1979), 572–573 (pointing out that the railroads were eager to help by providing discount fares to those going to see McKinley).

40. Morris, *Rise of Theodore Roosevelt*, 568; see ibid. at 573–575 (describing Roosevelt's campaign swing).

41. "They Fire on the Flag," *Chicago Tribune*, July 12, 1896, at 6; see Goodwyn, *Populist Moment*, 279 ("The massive national campaign for 'honest money' engineered by Mark Hanna set a model for twentieth-century American politics.").

42. See Brands, *Reckless Decade*, 273–274; see also Kazin, *Godly Hero*, 66 (pointing out that these leaflets were printed in several languages as part of the Republican outreach to immigrants).

43. See Act of Mar. 3, 1837, ch. 34, 5 Stat. 176.

44. *Campaign Text-Book of the National Democratic [Gold] Party*, 4 (quoting Chairman Bynum's address to the rump convention).

45. Ibid. at 9.

46. Ibid. at 22–23 (quoting the speech of Simon B. Bruckner).

47. Delmore Elwell, *A Wall Street View of the Campaign Issues of 1896* (New York: Published by the author, 1896), 3.

48. J. S. Barcus, *The Boomerang, or Bryan's Speech with the Wind Knocked Out* (New York: J. S. Barcus, 1896), 43.

49. "The Nation's Honor Must Be Preserved," *Harper's Weekly*, September 26, 1896, at 938; see "The Triumph of Socialism and Communism," *Harper's Weekly*, July 18, 1896, at 697 (stating that the Democratic Party "announces its readiness to make war upon the Supreme Court").

50. "Bryan and Sewell," *New York Times*, July 12, 1896, at 1.

51. Donald Grier Stephenson Jr., *Campaigns and the Court* (New York: Columbia University Press, 1999), 127.

52. *Republican Campaign Text-Book*, 139; see ibid. (quoting a prior statement by Bryan supporting term limits for the Justices).

53. Sylvester Pennoyer, "The Case of *Marbury v. Madison*," *American Law Review* 30 (1896): 201.

54. There is a popular myth that *The Wizard of Oz* (the book, not the movie) is a parable for the 1896 election. Under this reading, the Scarecrow represents farmers, the Tin Man symbolizes workers, Dorothy is the average voter (from Kansas), the Cowardly Lion is Bryan (all bark and no bite), and the Wizard is McKinley. (I am not clear who the Wicked Witch is supposed to be.) Moreover, the magic shoes that Dorothy wears are silver, the yellow-brick road evokes the gold standard, and the Emerald City is green because Washington is the color of money. This reading is clever, but there is no proof that L. Frank Baum, the author of the *Oz* series, had politics in mind.

55. See Jean Strouse, *Morgan: American Financier* (New York: Random House, 1999), 256 (discussing the Haymarket Riot).

56. William J. Bryan, *The First Battle: A Story of the Campaign of 1896* (Chicago: W. B. Conkey, 1896), 415.

57. Ibid. at 416.

58. Ibid. at 480.

59. See generally Joseph Alsop and Turner Catledge, *The 168 Days* (Garden City, NY: Doubleday, Doran, 1938) (describing the "switch-in-time" in 1937).

60. For a thoughtful discussion of how this readjustment occurred and its implications for judicial review, see Barry Friedman, *The Will of The People: How Public Opinion Has Influenced the Supreme Court and Shaped the Meaning of the Constitution* (New York: Farrar, Straus and Giroux, 2009), 212–236.

61. See Cherny, *Righteous Cause*, 69; see also Kazin, *Godly Hero*, 76 (putting the turnout rate at 79.3 percent).

62. Cherny, *Righteous Cause*, 70; see Sundquist, *Dynamics of the Party System*, 157.

63. See Kazin, *Godly Hero*, 76.

64. See Michael Klarman, *From Jim Crow to Civil Rights* (New York: Oxford University Press, 2004), 15.

65. Sundquist, *Dynamics of the Party System*, 158; see ibid. at 158–169 (providing a close analysis of the election returns).

66. In a sense, Bryan was the first in a long line of Democratic presidential candidates who could not forge a coalition between African Americans in the South and working-class whites in the North and the Midwest.

67. "The Week," *The Nation*, November 5, 1896, at 337.

SIX
A New Constitutional Regime

1. See New York Times v. Sullivan, 376 U.S. 254, 273–276 (1964) (discussing the history of the Alien and Sedition Act).

2. See Neal Katyal, "Sunsetting Judicial Opinions," *Notre Dame Law Review* 79 (2004): 1237–1256 (proposing such a remedy in national security cases).

3. As far as I can tell, there is no counterpart to this "green light" in any other generation.

4. Finley Peter Dunne, *Mr. Dooley's Opinions* (New York: R. H. Russell, 1901), 26. Dunne was talking about *Downes v. Bidwell*, which was decided after the 1900 presidential election and dealt with the extension of the Constitution to territories acquired in the Spanish-American War.

5. See United States v. Darby, 312 U.S. 100, 118 (1941) (holding that Congress had the power to ban child labor under the commerce power); Wickard v. Fillburn, 317 U.S. 111, 120 (1942) (stating that limits on the commerce power "must proceed from political rather than from judicial processes").

6. Chicago, 166 U.S. at 226. The Court held that the property dispute at issue did not constitute a taking, although Justice Brewer dissented on that question. See ibid. at 241–258; see also ibid. at 259 (Brewer, J., concurring in part and dissenting in part).

7. Ibid. at 241.

8. The only notable example was Pennsylvania Coal Co. v. Mahon, 260 U.S. 393 (1921), which invalidated a state law regulating coal mining because it went "too far." See ibid. at 415.

9. Allgeyer, 165 U.S. at 589.

10. Ibid. at 590.

11. See Adamson v. California, 332 U.S. 46, 80 (1947) (Black, J., dissenting) (explaining that *Allgeyer* "substantially adopted the rejected argument of counsel in the *Slaughter-House* cases, that the Fourteenth Amendment guarantees the liberty of all persons under 'natural law' to engage in their chosen business or vocation").

12. Davison M. Douglas, "The Rhetorical Uses of *Marbury v. Madison*: The Emergence of a 'Great Case,'" *Wake Forest Law Review* 38 (2003):

400; see ibid. at 401 (quoting another conservative lawyer, who said that "while the courts remain true to the example and precepts of Marshall, all the essential rights of the citizen are as secure as the earth under his feet—they can no more be invaded than the stars in heaven can be blotted from his gaze").

13. See ibid. at 398–399; ibid. at 399 (quoting one speaker's opinion that before *Marbury* "the popular notions a century ago were deeply tinctured with the doctrines and theories engendered by the French Revolution").

14. See Michael Gerhardt, "The Lives of John Marshall," *William and Mary Law Review* 43 (2002): 1412.

15. Douglas, "Rhetorical Uses," 399.

16. See ibid. at 398 n.99.

17. Citations to *Marbury* increased sharply after 1900. See ibid. at 404–407. It is also worth noting that the Court embraced *Gibbons* as the touchstone for analysis of the Commerce Clause in 1899. See Addyston Pipe & Steel Co. v. United States, 175 U.S. 211, 228 (1899).

18. This trend was given a boost by the Spanish-American War, which made America a colonial power and tended to legitimate the idea that there were superior and inferior races and that governing institutions should recognize that distinction.

19. See James L. Hunt, *Marion Butler and American Populism* (Chapel Hill: University of North Carolina Press, 2003), 154 (stating that by 1898 the Populists had "witnessed a critical weakening of their strength. The leading reason for decline, in North Carolina and in the nation, was the increasing irrelevance of Populist reform. At the national level, midroaders and cooperationists failed to resolve their differences or develop effective issues, while in North Carolina violence and white supremacy became the dominant political forces."); see also William Warren Rogers Sr., *The One-Gallused Rebellion: Agrarianism in Alabama, 1865–1896* (Tuscaloosa: University of Alabama Press, 2001), 332–333 ("In the regional context, the theory that the collapse of the Populist movement meant political oblivion for the Southern Negro seems valid.").

20. See Gene Clanton, *Populism: The Humane Preference in America, 1890–1900* (Boston: Twayne, 1991), 163 (describing the lawsuit brought challenging Topeka's segregated schools shortly after *Plessy*).

21. See C. Vann Woodward, *The Strange Career of Jim Crow*, rev. ed. (1955; repr., New York: Oxford University Press, 2002), 97–102. This was also backed by violence, for there was a notable upswing in race riots

against African Americans after 1896. See Joel Williamson, *The Crucible of Race: Black-White Relations in the American South since Emancipation* (New York: Oxford University Press, 1984), 195–209 (discussing some examples).

22. See Joseph Columbus Manning, *Fadeout of Populism* (New York: T. A. Hebbons, 1928), 49 ("The leaders of the Southern Democratic party turned to the ingenuity of devising state constitutions embodying suffrage clauses which have enabled the machinery of registration and election to dominate the question by the simple process of disenfranchisement of the greater portion of opposition voters."); Burton D. Wechsler, "Black and White Disenfranchisement: Populism, Race, and Class," *American University Law Review* 52 (2002): 29 ("In the ensuing assault on the ballot, the class and race of the quarry were intertwined.").

23. See Woodward, *Strange Career*, 83–85 (describing this trend); see also Davis Rich Dewey, *National Problems, 1885–1897* (New York: Greenwood, 1968), 172–173 (stating that Louisiana, North Carolina, Alabama, Maryland, and Virginia adopted constitutional suffrage restrictions between 1898 and 1902). Mississippi was the first to use these antidemocratic techniques in its 1890 constitution. See Dewey, *National Problems*, 171.

24. All of the voting statistics in this paragraph come from Richard H. Pildes, "Democracy, Anti-Democracy, and the Canon," *Constitutional Commentary* 17 (2000): 303–304.

25. See William E. Forbath, "Caste, Class, and Equal Citizenship," *Michigan Law Review* 98 (1999): 50 ("The poll tax proved a defining feature of the Jim Crow order forged around the turn of the century, and in many southern states far more whites than blacks—a majority of white voters—were barred from the ballot box by the tax.").

26. See Pildes, "Democracy, Anti-Democracy," 313 (stating that the North Carolina antisuffrage amendments passed with only 59 percent of the vote even though African Americans were almost entirely barred from the polls); ibid. at 316 (pointing out that the 1901 Alabama constitution only received 57 percent of the vote and would not have passed without massive fraud in the Black Belt counties).

27. Manning, *Fadeout of Populism*, 50.

28. C. Vann Woodward, *Tom Watson: Agrarian Rebel* (New York: Macmillan, 1938), 371; see Florence Emeline Smith, "The Populist Movement

and Its Influence in North Carolina" (Ph.D. diss., University of Chicago, 1929), 173–174 ("Many Populists were opposed to the [Florida voting] amendment, saying that it was unconstitutional, that it would disenfranchise nearly one fourth of the white men of the state, and that it would not settle the negro question."); see also Hunt, *Marion Butler*, 161–162 (documenting Butler's speech in the Senate attacking the North Carolina suffrage proposal).

29. Giles v. Harris, 189 U.S. 475 (1903); Pildes, "Democracy, Anti-Democracy," 317. The result in *Giles* was foreshadowed by Williams v. Mississippi, 170 U.S. 213 (1898), in which the Court rejected a facial challenge to that state's voting limits.

30. Brief for Appellee in Giles v. Harris, No. 493 at 8.

31. Giles, 189 U.S. at 486. Holmes gets a lot more attention for his dissents from the post-Populist order in the liberty-of-contract cases. *Giles*, however, did a lot more harm than the decisions that Holmes complained about.

32. Ibid. at 488. Justice Harlan dissented in *Giles*, although he confined his discussion to the jurisdictional issue in the case. See ibid. at 493–504; see also ibid. at 491 (Brewer, J., dissenting) (stating that "that such relief will be given has been again and again affirmed in both national and state courts").

33. See Pildes, "Democracy, Anti-Democracy," 310 (describing the 1904 decision by the House of Representatives to cease examining the credentials of members elected in districts where African Americans were excluded from voting). This points up the theme of chapter 7, which is that progressives such as Theodore Roosevelt did little to alter the constitutional law created by the Populist upheaval.

34. In fairness to Holmes, let me note that the Court had previously used a "lack of remedy" excuse to paper over generational divisions. See Marbury at 168–180 (holding that Marbury was not entitled to a remedy, in order to avoid a clash with the Jeffersonians); see also Ex Parte McCardle, 74 U.S. (7 Wall.) 506, 512–515 (1869) (holding that it did not have any jurisdiction to assess the validity of military rule in the South during Reconstruction).

35. See Alexander M. Bickel and Benno C. Schmidt Jr., *The Judiciary and Responsible Government, 1910–1921*, vol. 9 of *History of the Supreme Court of the United States* (New York: Cambridge University Press, 1984), 739 ("Flamboyant demagogues like Cole Blease, Theodore Bilbo, and,

in his tragic later years, Tom Watson rallied their mobs of frustrated white supporters with incendiary racial slanders of astonishing malevolence."). The full story of Watson's transformation from reformer to archconservative is told in Woodward, *Tom Watson.*

36. See Maxwell, 176 U.S. at 582.

37. Justice Harlan, the lone dissenter in *Maxwell,* rejected the distinction between substantive and procedural incorporation. See ibid. at 616 (Harlan, J., dissenting) ("The privileges and immunities specified in the first ten Amendments as belonging to the people of the United States are equally protected by the Constitution. No judicial tribunal has authority to say that some of them may be abridged by the states while others may not be abridged.").

38. See ibid. at 593 ("If all of these rights are included in the phrase 'privileges or immunities' of citizens of the United States, which the states by reason of the Fourteenth Amendment cannot in any manner abridge, then the sovereignty of the state in regard to them has been entirely destroyed, and the *Slaughter-House Cases* and *United States v. Cruikshank* are all wrong, and should be overruled.").

39. Ibid. at 591.

40. Ibid. at 614 (Harlan, J., dissenting). Justice Field, the lead dissenter in *O'Neil,* was dead by the time the Court decided *Maxwell.* My explanation does run into a problem in the sense that Harlan joined *Debs* and remained a proponent of incorporation, but nobody else took both positions.

41. See Sullivan, 376 U.S. at 256–265 (expanding First Amendment protection against state libel law for a newspaper advertisement in which a civil rights protest was discussed).

42. See Downes, 182 U.S. at 244; see also Hawaii v. Mankichi, 190 U.S. 197 (1903) (rejecting the argument that the Sixth Amendment right to trial by jury applied to the territory of Hawaii). For an interesting take on these decisions, see Christina Duffy Burnett, "Untied States: American Expansion and Territorial Deannexation," *University of Chicago Law Review* 72 (2005): 797–879.

43. Michael Kazin, *A Godly Hero: The Life of William Jennings Bryan* (New York: Alfred A. Knopf, 2006), 103.

44. Ibid. at 105.

45. Edmund Morris, *The Rise of Theodore Roosevelt* (New York: Modern Library, 1979), 771.

46. See Edmund Morris, *Theodore Rex* (New York: Random House, 2001), 97–101 (describing some aspects of the rebellion and the use of torture by some American soldiers).

The Progressive Correction

1. Richard Hofstadter, *The Age of Reform: From Bryan to FDR* (New York: Alfred A. Knopf, 1955), 94.
2. See Michael Kazin, *A Godly Hero: The Life of William Jennings Bryan* (New York: Alfred A. Knopf, 2006), 163 (noting that Bryan received just 43 percent of the popular vote in 1908).
3. See Akhil Reed Amar, *America's Constitution: A Biography* (New York: Random House, 2005), 405–430 (describing all of the Progressive amendments).
4. See, e.g., Ron Chernow, *Titan: The Life of John D. Rockefeller, Sr.* (New York: Random House, 1998), 551 ("The Progressive movement favored peaceful, incremental change and was infused with unimpeachable ideals: that people should be healthier and better educated and that government should operate in a businesslike manner. The Progressives conjured up an antiseptic world of public administration in which decisions would be made rationally by scholars, scientists, and experts.").
5. For an example of Roosevelt's international style, see Edmund Morris, *Theodore Rex* (New York: Random House, 2001), 402–414 (discussing his mediation of the Russo-Japanese War, for which he won a Nobel Peace Prize).
6. Roosevelt's political dilemma is explained brilliantly by Stephen Skowronek, *The Politics Presidents Make: Leadership from John Adams to Bill Clinton*, rev. ed. (1993; repr., Cambridge: Harvard University Press, 1997), 228–258.
7. See David E. Kyvig, *Explicit and Authentic Acts: Amending the U.S. Constitution, 1776–1995* (Lawrence: University Press of Kansas, 1996), 201 (noting that Taft expressed support for an income tax in his 1908 campaign).
8. See Knowlton v. Moore, 178 U.S. 41, 78–81 (1900) (upholding an estate tax enacted during the Spanish-American War and distinguishing *Pollock*).

9. See Michael Klarman, *From Jim Crow to Civil Rights* (New York: Oxford University Press, 2004), 68 (stating that the "political nadir of race relations at the national level may have come in the 1912 presidential election and its aftermath"); see also Alexander M. Bickel and Benno C. Schmidt Jr., *The Judiciary and Responsible Government, 1910–1921*, vol. 9 of *History of the Supreme Court of the United States* (New York: Cambridge University Press, 1984), 937–938 (explaining that Wilson broke with the post-Reconstruction tradition of an integrated civil service).

10. See Lochner, 198 U.S. at 45; Adair v. United States, 208 U.S. 161 (1908). The Justices did not strike down every statute that was challenged on due process grounds, of course. See Muller v. Oregon, 208 U.S. 412 (1908) (upholding an Oregon law that established maximum working hours for women).

11. Twining v. New Jersey, 211 U.S. 78, 98 (1908).

12. See Morris, *Theodore Rex*, 150–169 (discussing the president's role in settling the coal strike); see also Hofstadter, *Age of Reform*, 235 ("The most important year of his presidency was 1902, when he brought the great anthracite strike to a successful arbitration and launched the prosecution of the Northern Securities Company . . . They were symbolic acts of the highest importance.").

13. See Hofstadter, *Age of Reform*, 236 ("The psychological impact of the Northern Securities prosecution was comparable to that of the strike settlement, though the economic content was relatively meaningless."); Kazin, *Godly Hero*, 114 (noting that Bryan's newspaper, *The Commoner*, "charged the President with speaking loudly about the evils of trusts but rarely employing his prosecutorial stick—and never against his corporate friends"); see also United States v. Trans-Missouri Freight Ass'n, 166 U.S. 290, 313 (1897) (upholding the application of the Sherman Act to railroads); Northern Securities, 193 U.S. at 329 (opinion of Harlan, J.) (stating that under *E. C. Knight* a firm that "directly embraced interstate or international commerce . . . would then have been covered by the anti-trust act and would have been illegal").

14. See Northern Securities, 193 U.S. at 364–400 (White, J., dissenting) (reasoning that Congress was not empowered to regulate stock purchases in state firms engaged in interstate commerce); ibid. at 402–403 (Holmes, J., dissenting) ("If the act before us is to be carried out according to what seems to me the logic of the argument for the government,

which I do not believe that it will be, I can see no part of the conduct of life with which, on similar principles, Congress might not interfere."). The controlling opinion in *Northern Securities* was Justice Brewer's concurrence, which held that the Sherman Act only reached unreasonable restraints of trade. See Northern Securities, 193 U.S. at 361 (Brewer, J., concurring). This is the position that the Court eventually adopted in Standard Oil Co. v. United States, 221 U.S. 1 (1911) (breaking up John D. Rockefeller Sr.'s trust).

15. Morris, *Theodore Rex*, 435 (discussing the debate on the Hepburn Act.)

16. This is especially true if one accepts Kevin Phillips's argument that McKinley was planning to do many of the things that Roosevelt ended up doing. See Kevin Phillips, *William McKinley* (New York: Henry Holt, 2003), 136 ("The experts, businessmen, and labor allies largely selected by McKinley—not by Theodore Roosevelt, not by Woodrow Wilson—wound up laying out much of what would be the Progressive corporate and antitrust agenda through 1914."); cf. ibid. at 124 (stating that McKinley was considering an income tax in 1899). Since it is impossible to prove what McKinley would have done had he lived, I do not want to rely too much on this thought.

17. This was true in an intellectual sense as well. Charles Beard published his landmark book in 1913 arguing that the Constitution was an undemocratic structure designed from the outset to protect property rights. See Charles A. Beard, *An Economic Interpretation of the Constitution of the United States* (New York: Macmillan, 1913); see also Hofstadter, *Age of Reform*, 200 (stating that Beard's work "carried the Progressive mind to the inner citadel of the established order: a nation of Constitution-worshippers and ancestor-worshippers was confronted with a scholarly muckrucking of the Founding Fathers and the Constitution itself"). Beard's book is an excellent commentary on the backlash of the 1890s. The problem is that he incorrectly read those principles back into the original text.

18. Although the Seventeenth Amendment was enacted around the same time, it is not plausible to say that its success is attributable to Bryan's withdrawal from presidential politics. Pressure for popular Senate elections built gradually through petitions from various state legislatures for a constitutional convention on the issue. See Amar, *America's Constitution*, 410–412 (discussing the historical background). Moreover,

Senate elections were not central to the backlash against the Populist agenda in the way that income taxes were.

19. See David E. Bernstein, "*Lochner* Era Revisionism, Revised: *Lochner* and the Origins of Fundamental Rights Constitutionalism," *Georgetown Law Journal* 92 (2003): 10 ("In practice there was not one *Lochner* era but three. The first period began in approximately 1897 and ended in about 1911, with moderate Lochnerians dominating the Court. The second era lasted from approximately 1911 to 1923, with the Court, while not explicitly repudiating *Lochner*, generally refusing to expand the liberty-of-contract doctrine to new scenarios, and at times seeming to drastically limit the doctrine." (footnotes omitted)); see also Edward S. Corwin, *The Twilight of the Supreme Court: A History of Our Constitutional Theory* (New Haven: Yale University Press, 1934), 86 (stating that between 1910 and 1920 "the Court was generally dominated by a majority which was distinctly disinclined to interfere with state legislation on the basis of the Fourteenth Amendment, and whose members frequently asserted doctrine which to all practical intents and purposes was the doctrine of presumed constitutionality").

20. See Bickel and Schmidt, *Judiciary and Responsible Government*, 96 (stating of Taft that "his administration of the Sherman Act was markedly more vigorous, and less affected by 'gentlemen's agreements' than Theodore Roosevelt's"); see also American Tobacco Co. v. United States, 221 U.S. 106 (1911) (upholding a suit against the tobacco trust). The *American Tobacco* case was especially significant because it was hard to distinguish tobacco from sugar, the subject of *E. C. Knight*, for both were agricultural products that the firms refined.

21. See Standard Oil, 221 U.S. at 68. To be fair, the Justices had undercut *E. C. Knight* in earlier cases, but there was concern in some quarters that the Court would revive the decision.

22. See Bickel and Schmidt, *Judiciary and Responsible Government*, 13.

23. Morris, *Theodore Rex*, 73; see Bickel and Schmidt, *Judiciary and Responsible Government*, 13.

24. See Kazin, *Godly Hero*, 179–180; see also Bickel and Schmidt, *Judiciary and Responsible Government*, 4 ("The year 1910 was also something of a turning point in the political history of the country. It was a year of Republican insurgency . . . It saw Theodore Roosevelt's decisive turn to progressive agitation.").

25. Kazin, *Godly Hero*, 179.

26. Melvin I. Urofsky, *Louis Brandeis: A Life* (New York: Pantheon Books, 2009), 85; John Milton Cooper Jr., *Woodrow Wilson: A Biography* (New York: Alfred A. Knopf, 2009), 87.

27. See Phillips, *McKinley*, 126 ("Many, if not most of the Progressive crusaders had battled in the trenches against Bryan, including Robert La Follette, George Norris, Theodore Roosevelt, Jonathan Dolliver, William Allen White, Albert J. Beveridge, Louis Brandeis, and Woodrow Wilson. Only when the specters of Altgeldism and free silver vanished did they feel free to propose reforms again, or to indulge in crusades."); see also Hofstadter, *Age of Reform*, 132 (describing White's political evolution).

28. See Phillips, *McKinley*, 126.

29. Hofstadter, *Age of Reform*, 165.

30. See Phillips, *McKinley*, 129.

31. Eric Rauchway argues that McKinley's assassination by an anarchist, Leon Czolgosz, was the key event because it showed that compromise was necessary to avoid a social explosion. While I do not agree with Rauchway's view, his account of Czolgosz's trial is thoughtful. See Eric Rauchway, *Murdering McKinley: The Making of Theodore Roosevelt's America* (New York: Farrar, Straus and Giroux, 2003).

32. This idea of a backlash does not explain what occurred at the end of Wilson's term, when the pressures of World War I helped Prohibition and women's suffrage get ratified. I am also giving short shrift to Wilson's other reforms, such as the creation of the Federal Reserve, largely because I have to stop somewhere.

33. The other example of a second-order backlash is the Civil Rights Act of 1964, which Michael Klarman argues resulted from a backlash against southern white violence against protestors, which was itself a backlash against *Brown*. See Klarman, *From Jim Crow to Civil Rights*, 385–442 (discussing this thesis).

34. In this respect, Akhil Reed Amar's claim that the Progressive Era amendments expressed a new principle in support of income redistribution does not withstand scrutiny. See Amar, *America's Constitution*, 475. All the Sixteenth Amendment did was restore the law to where it was in 1895.

35. See Erik M. Jensen, "The Taxing Power, the Sixteenth Amendment, and the Meaning of 'Incomes,'" *Arizona State Law Journal* 33 (2001): 1110. A similar effort was stymied in the House of Representatives. See

Kyvig, *Explicit and Authentic Acts*, 201 (noting that Cordell Hull argued there that a constitutional amendment to overrule *Pollock* would not be ratified by the states).

36. 44 Cong. Rec. 1351 (1909) (statement of Sen. Bailey).

37. Ibid. at 1686 (statement of Sen. Beveridge). I live a few blocks away from what was Beveridge's old house in Indianapolis, so I have a particular interest in him.

38. Ibid. at 4022 (statement of Sen. Root).

39. Ibid. at 4115 (statement of Sen. Money).

40. Ibid. at 3446 (statement of Sen. Sutherland). The Four Horsemen were Justices Van Devanter, Sutherland, Butler, and McReynolds, who formed a bloc in opposition to most of Franklin D. Roosevelt's initiatives.

41. Ibid. (statement of Sen. Borah).

42. Ibid. at 3446–3447 (statement of Sen. Sutherland).

43. Ibid. at 3446 (noting a discussion between Senator Rayner and Senator Sutherland on this issue).

44. Presidential Message, Tax on Net Income on Corporations, S. Doc. No. 61–98, at 1–2 (1909).

45. Ibid. at 2.

46. See Bruce Ackerman, "Taxation and the Constitution," *Columbia Law Review* 99 (1999): 35 ("It was much easier to defend a corporate tax within the preexisting contours of constitutional doctrine.").

47. 44 Cong. Rec. 3992 (1909) (statement of Sen. Borah).

48. "The Corporation Tax," *New York Times*, July 4, 1909, at 6.

49. See Flint v. Stonetracy Co., 220 U.S. 107 (1911). The Court's decision may have been designed to take the air out of the amendment balloon, but there is no evidence to support this view.

50. Kyvig, *Explicit and Authentic Acts*, 205. Justice Brewer died before the Sixteenth Amendment was ratified.

51. The most obvious example is when one generation succeeds another and must decide which precedents should be discarded and which should be retained. Such a decision often requires a delicate determination of what constitutes settled law—which often includes law that is inconsistent with current preferences.

52. See United States v. Darby, 312 U.S. 100, 116–117 (1941) (upholding the abolition of child labor in the Fair Labor Standards Act and overruling *Hammer v. Dagenhart*).

Conclusion

1. See Michael Kazin, *A Godly Hero: The Life of William Jennings Bryan* (New York: Alfred A. Knopf, 2006), 263–264 (talking about the roots of Bryan's opposition to evolution).
2. Jacob E. Cooke, ed., *The Federalist* (Middletown, CT: Wesleyan University Press, 1961), 3.
3. The obvious flashpoint for this generation is the constitutionality of the individual health insurance mandate, which was part of the sweeping health-care bill enacted in 2010.
4. The connection would have been stronger if Bryan had won, of course, but his failure does not mean that there was no link between Populism and the New Deal.
5. For some background on the *Gold Clause Cases*, see David Glick, "Conditional Strategic Retreat: The Court's Concession in the 1935 *Gold Clause Cases*," *Journal of Politics* 71 (2009): 804–807.
6. See Norman v. Baltimore & Ohio R.R., 294 U.S. 240 (1935); Perry v. United States, 294 U.S. 330 (1935). The *Perry* case, which upheld the abrogation of gold clauses in United States bonds, was somewhat similar to *Giles* in its position that the government's action was unconstitutional but that no remedy could be given. Cf. Henry M. Hart Jr., "The Gold Clause in United States Bonds," *Harvard Law Review* 48 (1935): 1057 ("Few more baffling pronouncements, it is fair to say, have ever issued from the United States Supreme Court.").
7. The best account of Long's movement is Alan Brinkley, *Voices of Protest: Huey Long, Father Coughlin, and the Great Depression* (New York: Alfred A. Knopf, 1982). My research on "The Kingfish" is focused on his infringement of civil liberties in Louisiana and how federal constitutional law responded to his regime. See Gerard N. Magliocca, "Huey P. Long and the Guarantee Clause," *Tulane Law Review* 83 (2008): 1–44.
8. See Arthur M. Schlesinger Jr., *The Politics of Upheaval* (Boston: Houghton Mifflin, 1960), 45–46.
9. See Gerard N. Magliocca, "Court-Packing and the Child Labor Amendment," *Constitutional Commentary* 27 (2011).

Bibliography

BOOKS AND ARTICLES

Ackerman, Bruce. "Taxation and the Constitution." *Columbia Law Review* 99 (1999): 1–58.

———. *We the People.* 2 vols. Cambridge: Harvard University Press, 1991.

Adler, David Gray. "The Steel Seizure Case and Inherent Presidential Power." *Constitutional Commentary* 19 (2002): 155–213.

Akerlof, George A., and Robert J. Shiller. *Animal Spirits: How Human Psychology Drives the Economy, and Why It Matters for Global Capitalism.* Princeton, NJ: Princeton University Press, 2009.

Alsop, Joseph, and Turner Catledge, *The 168 Days.* Garden City, NY: Doubleday, Doran, 1938.

Amar, Akhil Reed. *America's Constitution: A Biography.* New York: Random House, 2005.

Arnett, Alex Mathews. *The Populist Movement in Georgia: A View of the "Agrarian Crusade" in the Light of Solid-South Politics.* New York: Columbia University, 1922.

Bibliography

Aynes, Richard L. "Constricting the Law of Freedom: Justice Miller, the Fourteenth Amendment, and the *Slaughter-House Cases*." *Chicago-Kent Law Review* 70 (1994): 627–688.

Bagehot, Walter. *The English Constitution.* 1872. Reprint, New York: Cosimo Classics, 2007.

Barcus, J. S. *The Boomerang, or Bryan's Speech with the Wind Knocked Out.* New York: J. S. Barcus, 1896.

Beard, Charles A. *An Economic Interpretation of the Constitution of the United States.* New York: Macmillan, 1913.

Bellamy, Edward. *Looking Backward, 2000–1887.* 1888. Reprinted with a preface by Walter James Miller. New York: Signet Classic, 2000.

Benton, Thomas Hart. *An Examination of the Dred Scott Case.* New York: D. Appelton, 1857.

Bernstein, David E. "*Lochner* Era Revisionism, Revised: *Lochner* and the Origins of Fundamental Rights Constitutionalism." *Georgetown Law Journal* 92 (2003): 1–60.

Bernstein, David E., and Ilya Somin. "Judicial Power and Civil Rights Reconsidered." *Yale Law Journal* 114 (2004): 591–657.

Bickel, Alexander M. "The Original Understanding and the Segregation Decision." *Harvard Law Review* 69 (1955): 1–65.

Bickel, Alexander M., and Benno C. Schmidt Jr. *The Judiciary and Responsible Government, 1910–1921.* Vol. 9 of *History of the Supreme Court of the United States.* New York: Cambridge University Press, 1984.

Black, Charles L. *A New Birth of Freedom.* New Haven: Yale University Press, 1999.

Bogen, David S. "*Slaughter-House* Five: Views of the Case." *Hastings Law Journal* 55 (2003): 333–398.

Bork, Robert H. *The Tempting of America.* New York: Free Press, 1990.

Brands, H. W. *The Reckless Decade: America in the 1890s.* New York: St. Martin's, 1995.

Brinkley, Alan. *Voices of Protest: Huey Long, Father Coughlin, and the Great Depression.* New York: Alfred A. Knopf, 1982.

Bryan, William J. *The First Battle: A Story of the Campaign of 1896.* Chicago: W. B. Conkey, 1896.

Burnett, Christina Duffy. "Untied States: American Expansion and Territorial Deannexation." *University of Chicago Law Review* 72 (2005): 797–879.

Burns, W. F. *The Pullman Boycott.* Saint Paul: McGill Printing Co., 1894.

Campaign Text-Book of the National Democratic Party. Chicago: National Democratic Committee, 1896.

Carstensen, Vernon Rosco, ed. *Farmer Discontent, 1865–1900.* New York: John Wiley and Sons, 1974.

Carwardine, William H. *The Pullman Strike.* 1894. Reprint, Chicago: Charles H. Kerr, 1973.

Chernow, Ron. *Titan: The Life of John D. Rockefeller, Sr.* New York: Random House, 1998.

Cherny, Robert W. *A Righteous Cause: The Life of William Jennings Bryan.* Norman: University of Oklahoma Press, 1994.

Clanton, Gene. *Populism: The Humane Preference in America, 1890–1900.* Boston: Twayne, 1991.

Clausewitz, Carl von. *On War.* 1832. Reprinted with a preface by Peter Paret, Michael Howard, and Bernard Brodie. Princeton, NJ: Princeton University Press, 1984.

Cooke, Jacob E., ed. *The Federalist.* Middletown, CT: Wesleyan University Press, 1961.

Cooley, Thomas M. *A Treatise on the Constitutional Limitations.* 1868. Reprint, New York: Da Capo, 1972.

Cooper, John Milton, Jr. *Woodrow Wilson: A Biography.* New York: Alfred A. Knopf, 2009.

Corwin, Edward S. "The *Dred Scott* Decision in the Light of Contemporary Legal Doctrines." *American History Review* 17 (1911): 52–69.

———. *The Twilight of the Supreme Court: A History of Our Constitutional Theory.* New Haven: Yale University Press, 1934.

Croly, Herbert. *Marcus Alonzo Hanna: His Life and Work.* New York: Macmillan, 1912.

Crosskey, William Winslow. *Politics and the Constitution in the History of the United States.* Vol. 2. Chicago: University of Chicago Press, 1953.

Curtis, Michael Kent. *No State Shall Abridge: The Fourteenth Amendment and the Bill of Rights.* Durham, NC: Duke University Press, 1986.

Dewey, Davis Rich. *National Problems, 1885–1897.* New York: Greenwood, 1968.

Douglas, Davison M. "The Rhetorical Uses of *Marbury v. Madison:* The Emergence of a 'Great Case.'" *Wake Forest Law Review* 38 (2003): 375–413.

Dunne, Finley Peter. *Mr. Dooley's Opinions.* New York: R. H. Russell, 1901.

Elwell, Delmore. *A Wall Street View of the Campaign Issues of 1896.* New York: Published by the author, 1896.

Farrelly, David G. "Justice Harlan's Dissent in the *Pollock* Case." *Southern California Law Review* 24 (1951): 175–182.

Faulkner, Robert P. "The Foundations of Noerr-Pennington and the Burden of Proving Sham Petitioning: The Historical-Constitutional Argument in Favor of a 'Clear and Convincing' Standard." *University of San Francisco Law Review* 28 (1994): 681–713.

Finkelman, Paul. "Civil Rights in Historical Context: In Defense of *Brown.*" *Harvard Law Review* 118 (2005): 973–1029.

Fiss, Owen M. *Troubled Beginnings of the Modern State, 1888–1910.* Vol. 8 of *History of the Supreme Court of the United States.* New York: Macmillan, 1993.

Forbath, William E. "Caste, Class, and Equal Citizenship." *Michigan Law Review* 98 (1999): 1–91.

Bibliography

Friedman, Barry. *The Will of the People: How Public Opinion Has Influenced the Supreme Court and Shaped the Meaning of the Constitution.* New York: Farrar, Straus and Giroux, 2009.

Fuller, Lon L. *Legal Fictions.* Stanford, CA: Stanford University Press, 1967.

Gaither, Gerald H. *Blacks and the Populist Movement: Ballots and Bigotry in the New South.* Tuscaloosa: University of Alabama Press, 2003.

Gerhardt, Michael. "The Lives of John Marshall." *William and Mary Law Review* 43 (2002): 1399–1452.

Gilman, Howard. *Constitution Besieged: The Rise and Fall of Lochner Era Police Powers Jurisprudence.* Durham, NC: Duke University Press, 1993.

Glenn, Norval D. "Distinguishing Age, Period, and Cohort Effects." In Jeylan T. Mortimer and Michael J. Shanahan, eds. *Handbook of the Life Course.* New York: Kluwer Academic/Plenum, 2003.

Glick, David. "Conditional Strategic Retreat: The Court's Concession in the 1935 *Gold Clause Cases.*" *Journal of Politics* 71 (2009): 800–816.

Goodwyn, Lawrence. *The Populist Moment: A Short History of the Agrarian Revolt in America.* New York: Oxford University Press, 1978.

Guthrie, Chris, Jeffrey J. Rachlinski, and Andrew J. Wistrich. "Blinking on the Bench: How Judges Decide Cases." *Cornell Law Review* 93 (2007): 1–43.

Hart, Henry M., Jr. "The Gold Clauses in United States Bonds." *Harvard Law Review* 48 (1935): 1057–1099.

Harvey, William H. *Coin's Financial School.* 1894. Reprinted with a preface by Richard Hofstadter. Cambridge: Harvard University Press, 1963.

Hicks, John D. *The Populist Revolt: A History of the Farmers' Alliance and the People's Party.* Lincoln: University of Nebraska Press, 1961.

Hofstadter, Richard. *The Age of Reform: From Bryan to FDR*. New York: Alfred A. Knopf, 1955.

Hughes, Charles Evans. *The Supreme Court of the United States, Its Foundation, Methods, and Achievements: An Interpretation*. Garden City, NY: Garden City Publishing Co., 1936.

Hunt, James L. *Marion Butler and American Populism*. Chapel Hill: University of North Carolina Press, 2003.

Irving, Edward. *Breakers Ahead! An Answer to the Question Where Are We At?* Stockton, CA: T. W. Hummel, 1894.

Jackson, Robert H. *The Struggle for Judicial Supremacy*. New York: Alfred A. Knopf, 1941.

Jefferson, Thomas. *The Papers of Thomas Jefferson*. Ed. Julian P. Boyd. 60 vols. Princeton, NJ: Princeton University Press, 1950–.

Jensen, Erik M. "The Taxing Power, the Sixteenth Amendment, and the Meaning of 'Incomes.'" *Arizona State Law Journal* 33 (2001): 1057–1158.

Jones, Francis R. "*Pollock v. Farmers' Loan & Trust Company*." *Harvard Law Review* 9 (1895): 198–211.

Jones, Stanley L. *The Presidential Election of 1896*. Madison: University of Wisconsin Press, 1964.

Jory, T. C. *What Is Populism? An Exposition of the Principles of the Omaha Platform Adopted by the People's Party in National Convention Assembled*. Salem, OR: Ross E. Moores, 1895.

Josephson, Matthew. *The Politicos, 1865–1896*. New York: Harcourt, Brace, 1938.

Katyal, Neal. "Sunsetting Judicial Opinions." *Notre Dame Law Review* 79 (2004): 1237–1256.

Kazin, Michael. *A Godly Hero: The Life of William Jennings Bryan*. New York: Alfred A. Knopf, 2006.

Kindleberger, Charles P., et. al. *Mania, Panics, and Crashes: A History of Financial Crises*. Hoboken, NJ: John Wiley and Sons, 2005.

Klarman, Michael. *From Jim Crow to Civil Rights.* New York: Oxford University Press, 2004.

Koenig, Louis W. *Bryan: A Political Biography of William Jennings Bryan.* New York: Putnam, 1971.

Kuhn, Thomas. *The Structure of Scientific Revolutions.* Chicago: University of Chicago Press, 1996.

Kyvig, David E. *Explicit and Authentic Acts: Amending the U.S. Constitution, 1776–1995.* Lawrence: University Press of Kansas, 1996.

Lane, Charles. *The Day Freedom Died: The Colfax Massacre, the Supreme Court, and the Betrayal of Reconstruction.* New York: Henry Holt, 2008.

LaRue, L. H. "Constitutional Law and Constitutional History." *Buffalo Law Review* 36 (1987): 373–401.

Letwin, William. *Law and Economic Policy in America: The Evolution of the Sherman Antitrust Act.* New York: Random House, 1965.

Levitt, Steven D., and Stephen J. Dubner. *Freakonomics: A Rogue Economist Explores the Hidden Side of Everything.* New York: William Morrow, 2005.

Lofgren, Charles A. *The Plessy Case: A Legal-Historical Interpretation.* New York: Oxford University Press, 1987.

Magliocca, Gerard N. *Andrew Jackson and the Constitution: The Rise and Fall of Generational Regimes.* Lawrence: University Press of Kansas, 2007.

———. "Court-Packing and the Child Labor Amendment." *Constitutional Commentary* 27 (2011).

———. "Huey P. Long and the Guarantee Clause." *Tulane Law Review* 83 (2008): 1–44.

———. "A New Approach to Congressional Power: Revisiting the *Legal Tender Cases.*" *Georgetown Law Journal* 95 (2006): 119–170.

Maier, Pauline. *American Scripture: Making the Declaration of Independence.* New York: Random House, 1997.

Manning, Joseph Columbus. *Fadeout of Populism.* New York: T. A. Hebbons, 1928.

Martin, Roscoe C. *The People's Party in Texas: A Study in Third Party Politics.* Austin: University of Texas, 1933.

Mayhew, David R. *Electoral Realignments: A Critique of an American Genre.* New Haven: Yale University Press, 2002.

McConnell, Michael W. "The Forgotten Constitutional Moment." *Constitutional Commentary* 11 (1994): 115–144.

Mead, James Andrew. "The Populist Party in Florida." Master's thesis, Florida Atlantic University, 1971.

Mitchell, Robert B. *Skirmisher: The Life, Times, and Political Career of James B. Weaver.* Roseville, MN: Edinborough Press, 2008.

Morris, Edmund. *The Rise of Theodore Roosevelt.* New York: Modern Library, 1979.

———. *Theodore Rex.* New York: Random House, 2001.

Nevins, Allan. *Grover Cleveland: A Study in Courage.* New York: Dodd, Mead, 1932.

Newsom, Kevin Christopher. "Setting Incorporation Straight: A Reinterpretation of the *Slaughter-House Cases.*" *Yale Law Journal* 109 (2000): 643–744.

Papke, David Ray. *The Pullman Case.* Lawrence: University Press of Kansas, 1999.

Peffer, William A. *Populism, Its Rise and Fall.* 1899. Reprinted with a preface by Peter H. Argersinger. Lawrence: University Press of Kansas, 1992.

Pence, Charles R. "The Construction of the Fourteenth Amendment." *American Law Review* 25 (1891): 536–550.

Pennoyer, Sylvester. "The Case of *Marbury v. Madison.*" *American Law Review* 30 (1896): 188–202.

Phillips, Kevin. *William McKinley.* New York: Henry Holt, 2003.

Pildes, Richard H. "Democracy, Anti-Democracy, and the Canon." *Constitutional Commentary* 17 (2000): 295–319.

———. "Keeping Legal History Meaningful." *Constitutional Commentary* 19 (2002): 645–651.

Pollack, Norman, ed. *The Populist Mind.* Indianapolis: Bobbs-Merrill, 1967.

Posner, Richard A. *An Affair of State.* Cambridge: Harvard University Press, 1999.

Post, Robert, and Reva Siegel. "*Roe* Rage: Democratic Constitutionalism and Backlash." *Harvard Civil Rights–Civil Liberties Law Review* 42 (2007): 373–433.

Primus, Richard A. *The American Language of Rights.* New York: Cambridge University Press, 1999.

———. "The Riddle of Hiram Revels." *Harvard Law Review* 119 (2006): 1680–1733.

Rabinowitz, Howard N. *Race Relations in the Urban South, 1865–1890.* Athens: University of Georgia Press, 1996.

Rauchway, Eric. *Murdering McKinley: The Making of Theodore Roosevelt's America.* New York: Farrar, Straus and Giroux, 2003.

Raustiala, Kal, and Christopher Sprigman, "The Piracy Paradox: Innovation and Intellectual Property in Fashion Design." *Virginia Law Review* 92 (2006): 1687–1777.

Republican Campaign Text-Book. Washington, DC: Hartman and Caddick, 1896.

Richardson, James D., ed. *A Compilation of the Messages and Papers of the Presidents, 1789–1897.* 10 vols. Washington, DC: Government Printing Office, 1899.

Ridge, Martin. *Ignatius Donnelly: The Portrait of a Politician.* Chicago: University of Chicago Press, 1962.

Rogers, William Warren, Sr. *The One-Gallused Rebellion: Agrarianism in Alabama, 1865–1896.* Tuscaloosa: University of Alabama Press, 2001.

Royall, William L. "The Fourteenth Amendment." *Southern Law Review* 4 (1878): 558–584.

Ryder, Norman. *The Cohort Approach: Essays in the Measurement of Temporal Variations in Demographic Behavior.* New York: Arno, 1980.

Schlesinger, Arthur M., Jr. *The Politics of Upheaval.* Boston: Houghton Mifflin, 1960.

Shesol, Jeff. *Supreme Power: Franklin Roosevelt vs. The Supreme Court.* New York: W. W. Norton, 2010.

Siegel, Reva B. "Constitutional Culture, Social Movement Conflict and Constitutional Change: The Case of the De Facto ERA." *California Law Review* 94 (2006): 1323–1419.

Silbey, Joel H., ed. *The American Party Battle: Election Campaign Pamphlets, 1828–1876.* 2 vols. Cambridge: Harvard University Press, 1999.

Skowronek, Stephen. *The Politics Presidents Make: Leadership from John Adams to Bill Clinton.* Rev. ed., 1993.; Reprint, Cambridge: Harvard University Press, 1997.

Smith, Florence Emeline. "The Populist Movement and Its Influence in North Carolina." Ph.D. diss., University of Chicago, 1929.

Smith, Rogers M. *Civic Ideals: Conflicting Visions of Citizenship in U.S. History.* New Haven: Yale University Press, 1997.

Stephenson, Donald Grier, Jr. *Campaigns and the Court.* New York: Columbia University Press, 1999.

Strouse, Jean. *Morgan: American Financier.* New York: Random House, 1999.

Sundquist, James L. *Dynamics of the Party System: Alignment and Realignment of Political Parties in the United States.* Washington, DC: Brookings Institute, 1983.

Taleb, Nassim Nicholas. *The Black Swan: The Impact of the Highly Improbable.* New York: Random House, 2007.

Thaler, Richard H., and Cass R. Sunstein. *Nudge: Improving Decisions about Health, Wealth, and Happiness.* New Haven: Yale University Press, 2007.

Bibliography

Tulis, Jeffrey K. *The Rhetorical Presidency.* Princeton, NJ: Princeton University Press, 1987.

Turner, Frederick Jackson. *The Frontier in American History.* New York: H. Holt, 1920.

Urofsky, Melvin I. *Louis D. Brandeis: A Life.* New York: Pantheon Books, 2009.

Watson, Thomas E. *The People's Party Campaign Book, 1892.* 1892. Reprint, New York: Arno Press, 1975.

Weaver, James B. *A Call to Action: An Interpretation of the Great Uprising, Its Sources and Causes.* Des Moines: Iowa Printing Co., 1892.

Wechsler, Burton D. "Black and White Disenfranchisement: Populism, Race, and Class." *American University Law Review* 52 (2002): 23–57.

Westin, Alan Furman. "The Supreme Court, the Populist Movement and the Campaign of 1896." *Journal of Politics* 15 (1953): 3–41.

Whicher, George F., ed. *William Jennings Bryan and the Campaign of 1896.* Boston: D. C. Heath, 1953.

Whittle, James Lowry. *Grover Cleveland.* London: Bliss, Sands, 1896.

Wildenthal, Bryan H. "The Lost Compromise: Reassessing the Early Understanding in Court and Congress on Incorporation of the Bill of Rights in the Fourteenth Amendment." *Ohio State Law Journal* 61 (2000): 1051–1173.

Williamson, Joel. *The Crucible of Race: Black-White Relations in the American South since Emancipation.* New York: Oxford University Press, 1984.

Wills, Garry. *Certain Trumpets: The Call of Leaders.* New York: Simon and Schuster, 1994.

Wilson, Woodrow. *Congressional Government: A Study in American Politics.* (1885) Reprint with a preface by Walter Lippmann. New York: Meridian Books, 1956.

Woodard, Douglas Dutro. "The Presidential Election of 1896." Master's thesis, Georgetown University, 1949.

Woodward, C. Vann. "Strange Career Critics: Long May They Persevere." *Journal of American History* 75 (1988): 857–868.

———. *The Strange Career of Jim Crow.* Rev. ed., 1955. Reprint, New York: Oxford University Press, 2002.

———. *Tom Watson: Agrarian Rebel.* New York: Macmillan, 1938.

CASES

Act of March 3, 1837, ch. 34, 5 Stat. 176.

Adair v. United States, 208 U.S. 161 (1908).

Adamson v. California, 332 U.S. 46 (1947).

Addyston Pipe and Steel Co. v. United States, 175 U.S. 211 (1899).

Allgeyer v. Louisiana, 165 U.S. 578 (1897).

American Tobacco Co. v. United States, 221 U.S. 106 (1911).

Barron v. Baltimore, 32 U.S. (7 Pet.) 243 (1833).

Bowman v. Chicago and Northwestern Railway Co., 125 U.S. 465 (1888).

Brown v. Board of Education, 347 U.S. 483 (1954).

Brown v. New Jersey, 175 U.S. 172 (1899).

Budd v. New York, 143 U.S. 517 (1892).

Butchers' Union Slaughter-House and Live-Stock Landing Co. v. Crescent City Live-Stock Landing and Slaughter-House Co., 111 U.S. 746 (1884).

Chicago, Burlington and Quincy Railroad Co. v. Chicago, 166 U.S. 226 (1897).

Civil Rights Cases, 109 U.S. 3 (1883).

Davidson v. New Orleans, 96 U.S. (6 Otto.) 97 (1878).

Downes v. Bidwell, 182 U.S. 244 (1901).

Dred Scott v. Sandford, 60 U.S. (19 How.) 393 (1857).

Edwards v. Elliott, 88 U.S. (21 Wall.) 532 (1874).

Eilenbacker v. District Court, 134 U.S. 31 (1890).

Ex Parte McCardle, 74 U.S. (7 Wall.) 506 (1869).

Ex Parte Spies, 123 U.S. 131 (1887).

Ex Parte Virginia, 100 U.S. 339 (1880).

Flint v. Stonetracy Co., 220 U.S. 107 (1911).

Gibbons v. Ogden, 22 U.S. (9 Wheat.) 1 (1824).

Giles v. Harris, 189 U.S. 475 (1903).

Hawaii v. Mankichi, 190 U.S. 197 (1903).

Heart of Atlanta Motel v. United States, 379 U.S. 241 (1964).

Hurtado v. California, 110 U.S. 516 (1884).

Hylton v. United States, 3 U.S. (3 Dall.) 171 (1796).

In re Commissioners of First Draining District, 27 La. Ann. 20 (1875).

In re Debs, 158 U.S. 564 (1895).

In re Jacobs, 98 N.Y. 98 (N.Y. 1885).

In re Kemmler, 136 U.S. 436 (1890).

Interstate Commerce Act, ch. 104, 24 Stat. 379 (1887).

Julliard v. Greenman, 110 U.S. 421 (1884).

Kidd v. Pearson, 128 U.S. 1 (1888).

Knowlton v. Moore, 178 U.S. 41 (1900).

Knox v. Lee, 79 U.S. (12 Wall.) 457 (1871).

Lochner v. New York, 198 U.S. 45 (1905).

Marbury v. Madison, 5 U.S. (1 Cranch) 137 (1803).

Maxwell v. Dow, 176 U.S. 581 (1900).

McElvaine v. Brush, 142 U.S. 155 (1891).

M'Culloch v. Maryland, 17 U.S. (4 Wheat.) 316 (1819).

Miller v. Texas, 153 U.S. 535 (1894).

Missouri v. Lewis, 101 U.S. (11 Otto.) 22 (1880).

Mugler v. Kansas, 123 U.S. 623, 660 (1887).

Muller v. Oregon, 208 U.S. 412 (1908).

Munn v. Illinois, 94 U.S. 113 (1877).

New York Times v. Sullivan, 376 U.S. 254 (1964).

Norman v. Baltimore and Ohio Railroad, 294 U.S. 240 (1935).

Northern Securities Co. v. United States, 193 U.S. 197 (1904).

O'Neil v. Vermont, 144 U.S. 323 (1892).

Pace v. Alabama, 106 U.S. 583 (1883).

Pacific Insurance Co. v. Soule, 74 U.S. (7 Wall.) 433 (1869).

Parents Involved in Community Schools v. Seattle District, 551 U.S. 701 (2007).

Pennsylvania Coal Co. v. Mahon, 260 U.S. 393 (1921).

Perry v. United States, 294 U.S. 330 (1935).

Plessy v. Ferguson, 163 U.S. 537 (1896).

Pollock v. Farmers' Loan and Trust Co., 157 U.S. 429 (1895), modified on rehearing, 158 U.S. 601.

Presser v. Illinois, 116 U.S. 252 (1886).

Reagan v. Farmers' Loan and Trust Co., 154 U.S. 362 (1894).

Rowan v. State, 30 Wis. 129 (Wis. 1872).

Scholey v. Rew, 90 U.S. (23 Wall.) 331 (1874).

Sherman Antitrust Act, ch. 647, 26 Stat. 209 (1890).

Slaughter-House Cases, 83 U.S. (16 Wall.) 36 (1873).

Springer v. United States, 102 U.S. 586 (1881).

Standard Oil Co. v. United States, 221 U.S. 1 (1911).

State ex rel. Walker v. Judge of Section A, Criminal District Court, 39 La. Ann. 132, 1 So. 437 (La. 1887).

State v. Bates, 14 Utah 293, 47 P. 78 (Utah 1896).

Stone v. Farmers' Loan and Trust, 116 U.S. 307 (1886).

Stone v. Wisconsin, 94 U.S. 181 (1877).

Strauder v. West Virginia, 100 U.S. 303 (1880).

Trade-Mark Cases, 100 U.S. 82 (1879).

Twining v. New Jersey, 211 U.S. 78 (1908).

United States v. Callender, 25 F. Cas. 239 (C.C.D. Va. 1800) (No. 14,709) (Chase, J.).

United States v. Cruikshank, 92 U.S. (2 Otto.) 542 (1876).

United States v. Darby, 312 U.S. 100 (1941)

United States v. E. C. Knight Co., 156 U.S. 1 (1895).

United States v. Lopez, 514 U.S. 549 (1995).

United States v. Trans-Missouri Freight Ass'n, 166 U.S. 290 (1897).

Veazie Bank v. Fenno, 75 U.S. (8 Wall.) 533 (1869).

Wabash, Saint Louis and Pacific Railway Co. v. Illinois, 118 U.S. 557 (1886).

Walker v. Sauvinet, 92 U.S. (2 Otto.) 90 (1876).

Wickard v. Fillburn, 317 U.S. 111 (1942).

Williams v. Mississippi, 170 U.S. 213 (1898).

Worcester v. Georgia, 31 U.S. (6 Pet.) 515 (1832).

Yick Wo v. Hopkins, 118 U.S. 356 (1886).

Index

Ackerman, Bruce, 29
Adair v. United States (1908), 137
Adams, Henry, 106
African Americans: and conservative backlash, 26, 117, 124–125; and Populism, 26, 28, 44–47; and *Slaughter-House Cases*, 15; voting rights of, 4–5, 64, 124–125, 130, 132, 151
Agrarian interests: Bryan's support for, 102; and Cleveland, 55; and conservative backlash, 117; and Democratic Party, 46; and Populism's rise, 34–35, 37–38
Alabama: African American voting rights in, 124, 125, 126; conservative backlash in, 125;

Jim Crow laws in, 65; minority rights in, 20–21; Populism in, 45, 65
Aldrich, Nelson, 139, 145
Alien and Sedition Act (1798), 118
Allen, William, 36
Allgeyer v. Louisiana (1897), 121, 122, 123, 129
Altgeld, John Peter, 57–58, 59, 93, 111
American Bar Association, 123
American Law Review on *Marbury*, 110–111
American Railway Union, 56
Antitrust regulation, 75, 138. *See also* Sherman Antitrust Act
Arkansas, Jim Crow laws in, 65

Article V process, 152–153
Asian Americans, 20
Availability heuristic, 30

Bagehot, Walter, 33, 149
Benton, Thomas Hart, 49
Beveridge, Albert, 142
Bill of Rights. *See* Incorporation
  of Bill of Rights
Borah, William, 143, 144, 145
Bradley, Joseph P., 13, 17
Brandeis, Louis, 139
Brewer, David, 19, 91, 92, 146
Brown, Henry, 86
Brown v. Board of Education
  (1954), 96–97
Bryan, William Jennings, 2;
  conservative backlash against,
  5; and Court-packing, 113; in
  election (1896), 2–3, 98–115;
  in election (1900), 2, 130–131;
  in election (1908), 2, 133;
  income tax bill sponsored
  by, 54, 77; vice presidential
  running mates, 98, 103–104,
  105
Bully pulpit, 135
Butler, Marion, 40, 41–42, 54,
  125

A Call to Action (Weaver), 40
Campaign finance for 1896 elec-
  tion, 98, 107–108
Cannon, Joseph, 139
Catholics, 39, 100

*Chicago, Burlington, and Quincy
  Railroad Co. v. Chicago* (1897),
  120
Chicago Tribune: on *Debs*, 90; on
  Harlan's dissent in *Pollock*, 86
Child Labor Amendment (pro-
  posed), 153
Choate, Joseph H., 78–79, 82,
  110, 146
Citizenship rights, 9–10, 14, 63
Civil disobedience, 55
Civil liberties, 62, 63
Civil Rights Act (1866), 10
Civil Rights Act (1875), 20, 21
Civil Rights Act (1964), 22
Civil Rights Cases (1883), 21, 23, 43
Clausewitz, Carl von, 50–51
Cleveland, Grover, 53; and
  Bryan's candidacy, 102; and
  Democratic Party, 104–105;
  and election (1892), 47, 48; and
  election (1896), 3; and Gold
  Democrats, 101–102; and
  Pullman Strike, 52–63, 71,
  87–94, 103
Coal strike (1902), 137
Coinage Act (1873), 33
Collective action, 36, 37
Commerce Clause: and con-
  servative backlash, 117, 122;
  incorporation of, 4; interpre-
  tation of commerce, 73–74;
  and Populism, 40–44, 52, 76;
  and Pullman Strike, 58, 60,
  71, 88–89

Index

Complacency, as symbol of long incumbency, 32
Conservative backlash: Cleveland as leader of, 48; and election (1896), 5, 106–107, 109; and Jim Crow laws, 65, 94, 96; and Pullman Strike, 61, 90
Constitutional amendments: Article V process, 152–153; and Progressivism, 134, 142–148. *See also specific amendments*
Constitutional review, 81, 83, 143, 150
Constitutions, state, 17
Contract rights: and Fourteenth Amendment, 4, 9, 16, 23; and state constitutions, 17; Supreme Court on, 120–123
Cooley, Thomas M., 17
Corporate interests and Populism, 34–35, 38
Corporate taxes, 145, 146
Corruption, as symbol of long incumbency, 32
Court-packing, 98–99, 103, 108–109, 111, 153
Coxey, Jacob, 55, 104, 111
Crop-lien plan, 34
Cruel and Unusual Punishments Clause, 18, 91, 132
Currency reform, 100. *See also* Gold standard; Silver issue

Darby. See United States v. Darby
Darrow, Clarence, 87, 89

Debs, Eugene V., 56–57, 58, 87, 93, 111
Debs. See In re Debs
Declaration of Independence, 40
Democratic Party: and election (1894), 67–68; and election (1896), 99–106, 108–109; and generational cycle, 31; and Populism, 46, 66, 99–106; and Progressivism, 139; and silver standard, 101
Direct democracy, 38, 134, 140
Direct Tax Clauses, 77–78, 83, 84, 122
Disenfranchisement, 5
Donnelly, Ignatius, 37, 104
Dormant Commerce Clause, 41, 74, 75, 88
Douglas, Davison M., 81, 82
Downes v. Bidwell (1901), 130
Dred Scott v. Sandford (1857), 39, 43, 71, 81, 118
Due Process Clause, 4, 9, 24, 120, 121
Dunne, Finley Peter, 119

E. C. Knight. See United States v. E. C. Knight
Eighteenth Amendment, 134
Eighth Amendment, 18, 91
Election (1892), 52, 66
Election (1894; midterm), 67–68
Election (1896), 98–115; and conservative backlash, 117–119; constitutional regime

231

Election (1896) (*continued*) following, 116–132; Populist Party in, 99–106; and realignment, 7, 114–115; and Supreme Court, 106–114; voter turnout in, 114

Election (1900), 130–131

Election (1908), 133

Election (1912), 135

Election (1936), 113

Electoral College, 38

Elites: and incorporation of Bill of Rights, 130; and Progressivism, 134; and property rights, 130; and Pullman Strike, 62, 90

Emerson, Ralph Waldo, 1, 7

Eminent domain, 4, 24, 120–121

Equal Protection Clause, 9, 15, 20, 72

Equal Rights Amendment, 49–50

Executive power, 135

Fair Labor Standards Act (1938), 148

Farmers' Alliance, 36, 39, 43, 65

Federalism: and Pullman Strike, 58, 60, 62; and Reconstruction, 8–9. *See also* Incorporation of Bill of Rights

Federalist No. 1 (Hamilton), 150

Feedback loop, 48

Field, Stephen J., 10, 11, 18, 69, 85

Fifteenth Amendment, 13, 44, 126

Fifth Amendment, 18

First Amendment, 91

Food safety regulations, 137

"Force Bill" (1890), 64

Foreign policy, 135

Founding Fathers, 1, 29, 62

Fourteenth Amendment, 3–4, 9–16, 63, 85. *See also* Incorporation of Bill of Rights

Free speech, 63, 91

"Front-porch" campaign strategy, 107

Fuller, Melville, 73, 123

Fund-raising for 1896 election, 98, 107–108

Fusionists, 99–106

Garfield, James, 111

Gender discrimination, 50

Generational cycle: and constitutional interpretation, 150; and Populism, 28, 29–33, 49–52; and Supreme Court, 69

Georgia: Jim Crow laws in, 65; Populism in, 45, 65

Georgia Bar Association, 123

Gibbons v. Ogden (1824), 42, 74, 75, 82

Giles v. Harris (1903), 125–126, 151

Gold Democrats, 101–104, 109, 139

Gold standard, 33–36, 40, 53–54, 151–152
Grandfather clause, 124
Grand jury indictment rule, 18
Grange Movement, 36
Grant, Ulysses S., 114
Greenback Party, 36
Guarantee Clause, 61
Guiteau, Charles, 111

Hamilton, Alexander, 150
Hanna, Mark, 107–108
Harding, Warren, 135
Harlan, John Marshall, 21; *E. C. Knight* dissent by, 75, 76; *Plessy* dissent by, 94–95; *Pollock* dissent by, 79, 83, 85, 86; on private property rights, 130; *Slaughter-House* dissent by, 19, 22
Harper's Weekly: on Bryan in 1896 election, 110, 111, 112; on Pullman Strike, 57
Harvard Law Review on *Pollock*, 84
Hay, John, 106
Haymarket Riot (1886), 111
Head/poll taxes, 78, 124
Hepburn Act (1906), 137
Hill, David, 102
Hindsight bias, 25
Hofstadter, Richard, 133
Holmes, Oliver Wendell, Jr., 126, 127

Hoover, Herbert, 31
Hughes, Charles Evans, 80, 146
Hylton v. United States (1796), 78, 84

Immigration, 38–39
Imperialism, 130–131
Income tax: Bryan's sponsorship of bill, 54, 77; and conservative backlash, 117, 118; in Democratic Party platform, 103; and Populist Party platform, 38, 40; and Progressivism, 136, 142–148; Supreme Court on, 76–87
Incorporation of Bill of Rights: and property rights, 92; and *Slaughter-House Cases*, 12–13; Supreme Court on, 4, 17–20, 23–24, 128–132
Inheritance tax, 136, 145, 146
In re Debs (1895), 56, 87–94
Interstate Commerce Commission, 43
Intimidation tactics, 66

Jackson, Andrew, 6, 33, 109
Jackson, Robert H., 69
Jefferson, Thomas, 6, 29
Jim Crow laws: as conservative backlash, 124–128, 130; institution of, 5; and Populism, 63–67; and Progressivism, 136; Supreme Court on, 23, 24

Judicial activism, 81. *See also*
    Preemptive opinions
Judicial error, 27
Judicial modesty, 71
Judicial review, 81, 83, 143, 150
Jurisdiction, 80
Jury nullification, 90
Jury trial rights, 14, 19, 89, 128

Kentucky, Jim Crow laws in, 65
Klarman, Michael, 25, 26
Knights of Labor, 56
Kuhn, Thomas, 30

Labor unions, 56, 132, 137
Legal Tender Cases (1870, 1871,
    1884), 43
Legislatures, state, 65
Liberty of contract, 4, 23–24,
    136, 138, 150. *See also* Contract
    rights
Liquor sales, state regulation of,
    16, 41
Literacy tests, 124
Lloyd, Henry Demarest, 45, 100
Lochner v. New York (1905), 23
Lofgren, Charles, 25, 26
London, Jack, 139
Long, Huey P., 152
Looking Backward (Bellamy),
    37, 91
Louisiana: African American
    registered voters in, 124; Jim
    Crow laws in, 65, 94
Lynchings, 66

Marbury v. Madison (1803), 4, 44,
    81–83, 123, 150
Marshall, John, 4, 42–43, 71, 74,
    79, 110, 123
Marshall, Thurgood, 96–97
Maryland, Populism in, 65
Maxwell v. Dow (1900), 14, 23,
    93, 128
Mayhew, David, 3
McKinley, William, 108; in elec-
    tion (1896), 3, 98, 105, 106–
    115; in election (1900), 130–
    131; and Progressivism, 140
M'Culloch v. Maryland (1819),
    43, 44
Median voter support, 49
Minority rights, 20–22. *See also*
    African Americans
Mississippi, Jim Crow laws in, 65
Money, Hernando D., 143
Morgan, J. P., 54
Mutual transformation, 48, 55,
    77, 85, 108

The Nation: on Bryan, 5; on
    Harlan's dissent in *Pollock*, 86;
    on McKinley victory in 1896
    election, 115; on Pullman
    Strike, 93
National citizenship rights, 9,
    13, 14
Nationalization of industry, 5,
    37, 40, 74, 117, 152
Nativism, 38
New Deal, 6, 53, 113, 151

New Orleans Daily Picayune on *Plessy*, 95

New York Times: on agrarian protests, 55; on Bryan in 1896 election, 106, 110; on corporate and inheritance taxes, 145–146; on Harlan's dissent in *Pollock*, 86; on income tax, 147

Nineteenth Amendment, 134

Norris, George, 139

North Carolina: African American registered voters in, 124; conservative backlash in, 125; Populism in, 65

Northern Securities v. United States (1904), 137

Obama, Barack, 6

Olney, Richard, 58

O'Neil v. Vermont (1892), 18, 91, 93

One-party control, 32

Organized labor, 56, 132, 137

Panic (1893), 48

Panic (1907), 139

Party: one-party control, 32; two-party system, 74. *See also specific parties by name*

Paterson, William, 78

Peckham, Rufus, 121, 122, 129–130

People's Party, 39

Petition Clause, 13

Philadelphia Press on Bryan in 1896 election, 106

Pildes, Richard H., 125–126

Plessy v. Ferguson (1896), 23, 24, 25, 94–97

Politics: analogy with warfare, 50–51; formation of political attitude, 31

Poll/head tax, 78, 124

Pollock v. Farmers' Loan and Trust Co. (1895), 76–87, 147

Populism: and Commerce Clause, 40–44, 58, 76; and election (1896), 99–106, 108–109; and federalism, 61; fusion vs. independence of party, 99–106; and generational cycle, 29–33, 49–52; and grass-roots discontent, 33–39; and Jim Crow laws, 63–67; and Progressivism, 135; and Pullman Strike, 52–63; and race relations, 44–47; resistance to, 48–68; rise of, 28–47

Precedent, 71, 84, 85, 122

Preemptive opinions, 51–52, 70–72, 77, 118

Primaries, all-white, 124

Privileges or Immunities Clause, 9

Progressivism, 133–148; and constitutional change, 142–148; and income taxes, 136, 142–148; and Theodore Roosevelt, 2, 134–138; as

Progressivism (*continued*)
second-order backlash, 138–
142
Prohibition, 134
Property rights: elevation of,
120–123; and federalism, 62,
92; and Fourteenth Amend-
ment, 4, 9, 16, 85; and Pullman Strike, 90; and state
constitutions, 17; Supreme
Court on, 120–123
Protestants, 39
Protests, 55
Public works programs, 55
Pullman Strike: and Commerce
Clause, 71; Democratic Party
criticisms of, 103; and Populism, 52–63; and Supreme
Court, 87–94
Pure Food and Drug Act (1906),
137

Race issues: and Fourteenth
Amendment, 20–22; and
Populism, 5, 44–47. *See also*
African Americans; Jim Crow
laws
Railroads: and Dormant
Commerce Clause, 41; and
federal rate regulation, 137;
and Jim Crow laws, 48, 64,
124; and Populism's rise, 37;
and state rate regulations,
16–17, 72–76, 117. *See also*
Pullman Strike

Reagan Revolution, 6, 32
*Reagan v. Farmers' Loan and Trust
Co.* (1894), 72–76, 121
Realignment, political, 3, 7,
114–115
Reconstruction, 8–27; and Fourteenth Amendment, 16–22;
Slaughter-House impact on,
9–16
Redistribution of wealth, 5, 152
Republican Party: and election
(1894), 67–68; and election
(1896), 106–107, 110, 114–115;
and generational cycle, 31;
and Populism's rise, 46; and
Progressivism, 139; and Pullman Strike, 61
Right to work, 12
Rockefeller, John D., 138
Roosevelt, Franklin D., 53, 69,
109, 113, 151–152
Roosevelt, Theodore, 136; and
election (1896), 107; in election (1912), 135; and Progressivism, 2, 133, 134–138; as vice
presidential candidate, 131
Root, Elihu, 143
Rural culture, 34, 35, 64, 105. *See
also* Agrarian interests

School segregation, 96, 124
Segregation: and conservative
backlash, 117, 124, 132; expansion of, 124–128; of federal
workforce, 136; of public

schools, 96, 124; Supreme
Court on, 23. *See also* Jim
Crow laws
"Separate but equal," 23, 94
Seventeenth Amendment, 134
Sewell, Arthur, 103–104, 105
Sherman, John, 43, 73
Sherman Antitrust Act (1890),
43, 73, 88, 137–138
Shiras, George, 123
Siegel, Reva, 49, 50, 58
Silver issue, 33–34, 100, 101, 105
Sixteenth Amendment, 134, 138,
146
Sixth Amendment, 14, 89, 128
Skowronek, Stephen, 3
Slaughter-House Cases: and
African Americans, 15; and
federalism, 62–63; and Four-
teenth Amendment, 9–16, 63;
and incorporation of Bill of
Rights, 12–13; and property
rights, 85
Southern Populism: and Jim
Crow laws, 48, 63–67; and
race relations, 44–47
Spanish-American War, 130–131
Springer v. United States (1881),
77, 84
*Standard Oil Co. of New Jersey v.
United States* (1911), 138
Stare decisis, 85, 96
State citizenship rights, 9–10,
14, 63
State constitutions, 17

State legislatures, 65
Steffens, Lincoln, 139
Strikes: coal strike (1902), 137;
Pullman Strike, 52–63, 71,
87–94, 103
Suffrage. *See* Voting rights
Sugar trust, 73, 88
Supreme Court, 69–97; on
Commerce Clause, 43–44; on
contract rights, 120–123; on
corporate taxes, 146; and election (1896), 106–114; on federalism, 62–63; on Fourteenth
Amendment, 3–4; and income
tax, 76–87; on incorporation
of Bill of Rights, 4, 17–20,
23–24, 128–132; and judicial
resistance, 70–72; Justices
as political appointees, 70;
"packing" it with partisans,
98–99, 103, 108–109, 111,
153; and Populist resistance,
94–97; preemptive opinions
by, 70–72; on property rights,
120–123; and Pullman Strike,
56, 87–94; on segregation,
124–128. *See also specific cases
and Justices*
Sutherland, George, 143–144
Switch-in-time, 113–114, 119,
120, 148

Taft, William Howard, 133, 135,
138, 144, 145, 146
Takings Clause, 4, 24, 120–121

Taney, Roger, 71
Taxes: corporate, 145, 146;
    Direct Tax Clauses, 77–78, 83,
    84, 122; head/poll tax, 78, 124;
    inheritance, 136, 145, 146. *See
    also* Income tax
Tennessee, Jim Crow laws in, 65
Texas: Jim Crow laws in, 65;
    Populism in, 65; railroad rate
    regulation by, 72
Thirteenth Amendment, 13, 78,
    118
Tillman, Ben, 111
Trade-Mark Cases (1879), 43
Truman, Harry, 83
Trumbull, Lyman, 87, 89
Trusts: and Populism's rise, 35,
    42, 75; and Sherman Act,
    73, 88
Turner, Frederick Jackson, 34
Two-party system, 67

Unions, 56, 132, 137
United States v. Darby (1941), 120
United States v. E. C. Knight
    (1895), 72–76, 88, 89, 137
Urban voters, 39, 105

Virginia, African American reg-
    istered voters in, 124
Vote fraud, 38, 66, 125
Voter turnout, 114

Voting rights: for African Ameri-
    cans, 4–5, 64, 124–125, 130,
    132, 151; for women, 38, 134,
    140

Warfare and politics analogy,
    50–51
Warren, Earl, 96
Watson, Thomas E.: on Cleve-
    land administration, 54–55;
    and conservative backlash,
    125; on corporate interests,
    35; and Democratic Party,
    99–100; on immigration,
    38–39; as senator, 128; on
    southern Populism, 44, 66, 67;
    as vice presidential candidate,
    104, 105
Wealth redistribution, 5, 152
Weaver, James B., 39–40, 41, 42,
    47, 76, 99–101
West Virginia, African Ameri-
    cans serving on juries in, 20
White, Edward, 84
White, William Allen, 139
White primaries, 124
Wickard v. Fillburn (1942), 120
Wilson, Woodrow, 133, 135, 136,
    139
Women's suffrage, 38, 134, 140
Woodward, C. Vann, 22, 26
Worcester v. Georgia (1832), 71